Risk Management Issues in Insurance

Risk Management Issues in Insurance

Trends in Best Practice

Edited by
Martin Bird and Tim Gordon

First published in 2013 by

Bloomsbury Information Ltd
50 Bedford Square
London
WC1B 3DP
United Kingdom

Bloomsbury Publishing, London, New Delhi, New York, and Sydney
www.bloomsbury.com

A CIP record for this book is available from the British Library.

Standard edition	*Middle East edition*	*E-book edition*
ISBN-10: 1-84930-065-8	ISBN-10: 1-84930-066-6	ISBN-10: 1-84930-067-4
ISBN-13: 978-1-84930-065-0	ISBN-13: 978-1-84930-066-7	ISBN-13: 978-1-84930-067-4

Project Director: Conrad Gardner
Project Manager: Ben Hickling
Commissioning Editor: Lizzy Kingston

Typeset by Marsh Typesetting, West Sussex, UK
Printed and bound by CPI Group (UK) Ltd, Croydon, CR0 4YY

Contents

Introduction

The development of risk management is fascinating to watch. In theory, the interaction between providers and purchasers of risk, risk takers, and regulators results in a better understanding of different risks and their costs. That in turn enables our financial system to redistribute risks to those best able to take them. In practice, learning involves mistakes, and mistakes in risk management can be extremely painful. We are, of course, living through one right now. Poor regulation of systemic risk combined with the subprime mortgage crisis sent ripples—in some cases, tsunamis—to the far reaches of the global financial system. If nothing else, we hope the crisis has flushed out some of the complacency that allowed extreme risks to be assumed away and has re-focused minds on how best to manage risk in the future.

At one time, value at risk (VaR) was hailed as the magic bullet for risk management. Indeed, it lies at the heart of Solvency II for EU insurers. VaR can be a useful metric, but its fitness for purpose goes hand-in-hand with a set of implicit assumptions, one of which is that that the distributions of outcomes at the chosen level of significance is indicative of risks at other levels of significance. This is not always the case: risks that are unlikely to materialize but that have extreme consequences can easily slip through the VaR net.

There are varying responses to narrow risk measures such as VaR. On the one hand, sometimes we are stuck with it and have to do the best we can. For instance, Solvency II mandates VaR as *the* risk measure. The chapter by Stephen Richards develops a rational VaR framework that works within this constraint. In his chapter on market risk for insurers, Patrick Kelliher also aims to work with what is available in order to address the risks posed to insurers by market movements. He emphasizes that the important thing is that market risk *is* addressed, not the detail of *how* it is addressed.

On the other hand, sometimes complexity must be embraced, which is the tack taken by Neil Cantle and George Orros in their chapters. They are both concerned to ensure that insurers' assessments of risk are neither too narrow nor too simplistic. Cantle goes to some length to make the points that the manifestation of risk can be complex and that simple mathematical models can only go so far when dealing with complex systems populated by intelligent agents. In particular, complex systems can have emergent, highly nonlinear properties that cannot be modeled by breaking the whole into its (apparent) constituent parts and that, sometimes, it is the emergent properties that matter. Orros reviews enterprise risk management both in general and by reference to case studies (in which slavish reliance on VaR emerges as one of the factors in LTCM's downfall). A common theme here is that trying to understand difficult to model risks is necessary. They both note a certain fuzziness: Orros that what "good ERM" means is not generally understood and Kelliher that "market risk" is not itself well defined. But this is no different from modeling in general: tractable models are generally to be preferred, but only if they capture the essential aspects of what is being modeled.

Longevity risk, specifically longevity trend risk, is a case in point. Two approaches are possible: either fit a model to the past, or try to understand current and possible future drivers and use this to predict the future. They are both problematic. The modeling the past approach is short on the data required to model the long term realistically. This is because, as longevity improves, the medical and societal drivers of past longevity improvement will, by definition, fall away and so future improvement will depend on different drivers for which we, inevitably, have little or no data. This means that longevity improvement data from, say, 20 years ago, can be only weakly predictive of future longevity improvement and that calibration and backtesting have limited value. But at least we can test this type of model. The alternative, i.e. model individual causes of death or rely on expert predictions for these, makes for an entertaining story. But breaking down mortality by cause and attempting to model these individually reduces robustness because of sensitivity to the interactions between the causes, and we usually have poor or no data for this. This is similar to Cantle's concern that modeling a complex system by subcomponent can miss out on the potentially more important emergent properties. And the record of past expert predictions of future longevity improvement is dismal. Richards's framework for determining VaR demonstrates one advantage of the model fitting approach: because it starts with a well-defined statistical framework, it can relatively easily and consistently be adapted to produce a variety of statistical output.

In the United Kingdom, uncertainty over future longevity improvement combined with its financial impact (and a system of governance that is strong relative to most overseas locales) has led some UK pension plans to address longevity risk using longevity swaps, as covered by Bird and Gordon. In some cases, these pension plans are taking a meta view; not all of their advisers have considered longevity much of a risk. But the pension plans have noted that, at each triennial valuation over the past decade or so, these same advisers' best estimate longevity predictions have usually increased materially.

The chapter by Grimley covers bulk annuities, which remove all risk rather than specifically longevity risk. Grimley notes that being prepared in advance for transacting can be critical because when favorable market conditions do emerge, there can be a rush to buy. In 2008, only a small proportion of UK pension plans were nimble enough to take advantage of the very favorable terms that were available at that time.

Anthropomorphic climate change may be contentious, but what is not contentious is the impact that, for example, the severe 2011 floods in Thailand had on the global supply of hard disk drives and on the wider IT industry, all the way up to Intel failing to meet its quarterly revenue targets. Extreme weather events should come as no more of a surprise than market crashes—they have happened before and will happen again. In a world with ever more complex supply chains and interdependencies, the need to understand and manage weather-related risks is greater than ever. The chapter by Bernhardt, Havlicek and Drawas contends that the frequency and severity of weather catastrophe events is itself increasing and that many risk models are faulty because they assume a constant hazard rate. They also note that, although the reinsurance industry itself has addressed these concerns, there is a growing worldwide gap between economic weather catastrophe losses and the insured cover taken out for such losses. Hopefully, the topicality of "climate change" may make it easier to get this subject onto corporate risk agendas.

Finally, we note that although this book covers a variety of issues in connection with risk management, a common theme is that we still have a lot to learn. There is always something new in risk management.

We'd like to thank Conrad Gardner and Ben Hickling at Bloomsbury for their hard work and persistence in putting this book together.

Martin Bird and Tim Gordon (editors)

Contributor Biographies

Paul Barrett is AIG's EMEA chief operating officer for ERM. He is responsible for the risk management operations in the company, with a central analytics and governance team, plus risk officers reporting to him from key countries and hubs across EMEA. He has been leading on the development of the ORSA, Risk Appetite Framework, Risk Register, and governance processes, and leads the independent validation exercise for the internal model. Until July 2013 he also fulfilled the role as head of operational risk for AIG Europe. Previously he was assistant director, Solvency II at the Association of British Insurers. Prior to that he worked at the Financial Services Authority.

Alex Bernhardt founded Guy Carpenter's GC Micro Risk Solutions® division after the receipt of an Innovation Grant from the Microinsurance Innovation Facility housed at the International Labour Organization. Under his leadership, GC Micro has become a leading international development consultancy in the area of disaster risk management, helping development banks and public entities worldwide to manage climate-related risks affecting vulnerable populations. Mr Bernhardt regularly contributes to industry publications and speaks at industry events. He has obtained several AICPCU designations and is an honors graduate of the University of Puget Sound.

Martin Bird is a partner at Aon Hewitt and head of Aon Hewitt's risk settlement practice, which specializes in providing strategic risk management and longevity advice to a range of large UK and multinational clients with pension plans ranging in size from £50 million to over £30 billion. This includes structuring risk transfer transactions, advising on the value for money of different types of solution, and identifying which solutions provide the best fit to client objectives. He has led a number of high-profile longevity risk transfer transactions, including the BMW, BAE Systems, Rolls-Royce, and Pilkington deals, each of which covered £1 billion or more of pension liabilities.

David Blake is director of the Pensions Institute at Cass Business School and chairman of Square Mile Consultants, a training and research consultancy in London. He is also codesigner of the PensionMetrics lifecycle financial planning software; coinventor of the Cairns–Blake–Dowd stochastic mortality model; and cofounder with JPMorgan of the LifeMetrics indices. In 2011 he won the Robert I. Mehr award from the American Risk and Insurance Association for his paper on mortality risk transfers. The paper stimulated development of a new global capital market in mortality risk transfers between pension funds, life assurers, and capital market investors, leading to the world's first pension buy-out in 2006 and first pension buy-in and longevity swap in 2007.

Tom Boardman has over 35 years' experience of working in the financial services industry. He has an MA in economics from Cambridge University and is a fellow of the Institute of Actuaries. He left Prudential plc, where he was director of retirement strategy and innovation, at the end of March 2010 to become a trustee of the United Kingdom's National Employment Savings Trust (NEST) and a senior advisor at the Financial Services Authority. He is an honorary visiting professor at the Pensions Institute at Cass Business School.

Daniel Byrne is a risk analyst within the ERM department at AIG Europe Ltd. He specializes in developing and embedding key aspects of AIG Europe's risk management framework, including Risk Appetite, Own Risk and Solvency Assessment, Internal Model Uses, and Stress and Scenario Testing. Prior to this role he was the lead subject matter expert for the AIG Solvency II program. He had previously worked on the FSA Solvency II program, implementing Solvency II into the Supervisory Framework. He holds a BSc in economics from the London School of Economics.

Andrew Cairns is professor of financial mathematics at Heriot-Watt University, Edinburgh. He is a fellow of the Faculty of Actuaries and an active member of the UK and international actuarial profession. He is editor-in-chief of *ASTIN Bulletin*, the journal of the International Actuarial Association. His research interests concern the risk management of long-term life insurance and pension risks, most recently focusing on the modeling, measurement, and management of longevity risk.

Neil Cantle is a principal working in the London office of Milliman. He is a qualified actuary with over 20 years' experience working in the financial services and risk management industry. He leads the development of Milliman's CRisALIS approach to ERM, using insights from complexity sciences to deliver practical methods for modern risk management. In 2012 he led a research project in conjunction with the Universities of Bristol and Bath on behalf of the UK actuarial profession to apply complexity science to risk appetite and emerging risk. Cantle is one of 10 UK actuaries to have received the Chartered Enterprise Risk Analyst (CERA) designation as a thought leader.

Andy Davies joined Terra Nova in 1994 as group financial controller of Terra Nova Bermuda Holdings. In 2000 he became finance director at Markel International, with responsibility for reporting into Markel Corporation and overseeing the operations of the finance and RAO departments.

Neal M. Drawas is a senior consultant with MMA/Faulkner & Flynn, and consults on the development of operational management programs pertaining to sustainability, environmental health and safety, public reporting, compliance assessment, and internal due diligence. Mr Drawas's experience includes examination of existing programs to determine appropriate levels of operational control, resource adequacy, plan content, procedural effectiveness, and subsequent support in developing practical solutions for sustainable operating practices, environmental and social stewardship, and business continuity. He has an MS in engineering and a BA in biological sciences from Northeastern University.

Tim Gordon is a partner at Aon Hewitt and leads the Aon Hewitt longevity modeling team, which provides the mortality analysis and risk advice to support Aon Hewitt's UK funding and valuation actuarial advice and its longevity risk transfer transaction advice to pension plans and their sponsors, as well as to reinsurers of longevity risk. He developed and implemented Aon Hewitt's postcode and stochastic projections longevity models. He is currently chairman of the Continuous Mortality Investigation (CMI) of the UK actuarial profession, the body responsible for producing standard actuarial mortality tables and projections in the country.

Dominic Grimley manages bulk annuity broking for Aon Hewitt's Risk Settlement Group. His experience includes transactions of all shapes and sizes, from £1M buy-outs and buyins to deals of up to a £1bn to date, including accelerated transfers to support corporate transactions and a wide range of insolvency situations. Settlements so far include those for the Thorn, Leyland DAF, Powell Duffryn, and Motor Industry schemes. Dominic has advised on UK pensions since 1991 and transacted annuities since the late 1990s. He is a fellow of the Institute and Faculty of Actuaries, and of the Pensions Management Institute.

Stephen Haddrill became chief executive officer of the Financial Reporting Council in November 2009. Previously he was director general of the Association of British Insurers. He is a member of the Financial Crisis Advisory Group, the high-level advisory group set up by the IASB and the FASB to consider post-crisis financial reporting issues. From 2007 to 2011, he was vice president and chair of the board of the Institute for Employment Studies. Prior to that he held positions at the Department of Trade and Industry, including director general, Fair Markets Group, where he was responsible for the development of the framework within which business operates. He studied history and economics at Oxford University.

Tanya D. Havlicek is an associate actuary at Marsh Global Captive Solutions, assessing how climate change affects insurance coverage. Ms Havlicek is a member of the Casualty Actuarial Society, the Canadian Institute of Actuaries, the Society of Actuaries, and the American Academy of Actuaries' Property/Casualty Extreme Events Committee, studying climate change impacts to financial risk management. She holds a BSc in theoretical mathematics from Ohio State University and an MSc from the Nelson Institute for Environmental Studies at the University of Wisconsin-Madison. She has coauthored and peer reviewed numerous scientific journal articles, and led commissioning committees to support and perform research on climate change and assess the potential for the insurance industry.

Patrick Kelliher FIA is managing director of Crystal Risk Consulting Ltd., an independent risk consultancy based in Edinburgh. He was previously Head of Market Risk and ALM at Aegon UK. All told he has 25 years' experience of the life insurance industry including 10 years in risk management and consulting. A qualified actuary, he is a member of the Institute and Faculty of Actuaries ERM Thought Leadership committee and has authored/co-authored Actuarial profession papers and articles on topics as diverse as risk classification, liquidity risk and the difference between life insurance and banking risks.

Gene C. Lai is Safeco distinguished professor of insurance and chairperson of the Department of Finance, Insurance, and Real Estate at Washington State University. His publications have appeared in many journals, including the *Journal of Risk and Insurance*. Professor Lai has won numerous best paper awards, including one from the Casualty Actuarial Society. He serves as a coeditor for the *Journal of Insurance Issues* and as associate editor for many other journals, including the *Journal of Risk and Insurance*. He is vice president of the American Risk and Insurance Association (ARIA).

Morton Lane is director of the Master of Science in Financial Engineering program at the University of Illinois. He is also an independent consultant and president of Lane Financial, LLC, a broker-dealer operating at the intersection of the reinsurance and capital markets. Previously, he has been president of Sedgwick Lane Financial, senior managing director of the capital markets division at Gerling Global Financial Products, president of the Discount Corporation of New York Futures, senior managing director and head of commodities at Bear Stearns & Co., president of Lind-Waldock, investment officer for the World Bank, and lecturer at the London Graduate School of Business Studies. He has been awarded the Charles A. Hachemeister prize and has a PhD from the University of Texas.

S. Erik Oppers is deputy chief of the Global Financial Stability Division at the IMF. He leads research and writing teams that contribute to the Global Financial Stability Report, and works on a wide range of financial sector policy issues, including country financial sector assessments. In previous assignments at the IMF, he worked on Fund programs in Asia and financial sector issues and technical assistance in Africa. He earned a PhD in economics from Harvard University in 1993 and was assistant professor of economics at the University of Michigan, Ann Arbor, before joining the IMF in 1995. He served as head of control and finance (CFO) of the Netherlands Authority for the Financial Markets between 2003 and 2007.

George C. Orros is a freelance consulting actuary and general management consultant, specialising in the general, health, social care and life insurance industries. In 1993, following many years in insurance line management and in a global consultancy practice, he co-founded an actuarial and general management consultancy firm, which has offered actuarial, management consultancy and project management services to the insurance and financial services industry, both in the UK and internationally. He has extensive experience of strategic management, innovation, ERM and Solvency II regulatory developments, both as a project director and a technical expert. He is an accomplished author, communicator and speaker, with over 110 publications and numerous presentations.

Stephen J. Richards is a director of Longevitas Ltd, a company providing analytical software for mortality, longevity, and other demographic risks. The business spans the United Kingdom, the United States, Germany, and Australia, with users of the software including insurers, reinsurers, consulting actuaries, and regulators. He is a fellow of the Faculty of Actuaries in the UK and he holds a PhD from Heriot-Watt University, where he is also an honorary research fellow. He is an adviser to the CMI's Technical Committee in the UK and is an active researcher on the application of modern statistical techniques to business problems faced by life insurers.

Suzanne White, FCII, is chief executive officer of JWZ Solutions. Before founding JWZ Solutions, Dr White's most recent position was at a banking and finance institute in the Gulf, where, in addition to leading the insurance and accounting teaching teams, she was involved in other projects for the Chartered Insurance Institute as a member of the senior management team. A major responsibility and achievement was to establish the CII Academy at the Bahrain Institute of Banking and Finance (BIBF). Dr White has over 15 years of consultancy and training experience with educational and corporate entities, and she holds a PhD in educational research.

A Value-at-Risk Framework for Longevity Trend Risk

by Stephen J. Richards

This Chapter Covers

- Longevity risk faced by annuity portfolios and defined-benefit pension schemes is typically long-term, i.e. the risk is of an adverse trend which unfolds over a long period of time.

- However, there are circumstances in which it is useful to know by how much expectations of future mortality rates might change over a single year.

- Such an approach lies at the heart of the one-year, value-at-risk view of reserves, and also for the pending Solvency II regime for insurers in the European Union.

- This chapter describes a framework for determining how much a longevity liability might change based on new information over the course of one year.

- It is a general framework and can accommodate a wide choice of stochastic projection models, thus allowing the user to explore the importance of model risk.

Introduction

"Whereas a catastrophe can occur in an instant, longevity risk takes decades to unfold."

The Economist (2012)

Longevity risk is different from many others faced by insurers and pension schemes because the risk lies in the long-term trend taken by mortality rates. However, although longevity is typically a long-term risk, it is often necessary to pose questions over a short-term horizon, such as a year.

Two useful questions in risk management and reserving are "what could happen over the coming year to change the best-estimate projection?" and "by how much could a reserve change if new information became available?" The pending Solvency II regulations for insurers and reinsurers in the European Union are concerned with reserves being adequate in 99.5% of situations that might arise over the coming year. Insurers already have to do this as part of the Individual Capital Assessment (ICA) regime in the United Kingdom.

This chapter describes a framework for answering such questions, and for setting reserve requirements for longevity risk based on a one-year horizon instead of the more natural long-term approach. The chapter draws heavily on the paper by Richards *et al.* (forthcoming). The framework presented here is general, and can work with any stochastic projection model which can be fitted to data and is capable of generating sample paths. As with previous work in this area, such as Börger (2010), Plat (2011), and Cairns (2011), we will work with all-cause mortality rates rather than with rates disaggregated by cause of death.

In considering the insurer solvency capital requirement (SCR) for longevity risk, Börger (2010) concluded that "the computation of the SCR for longevity risk via the VaR approach obviously requires stochastic modelling of mortality." Similarly, Plat (2011) stated that "naturally this requires stochastic mortality rates." This chapter therefore only considers stochastic mortality as a solution to the value-at-risk (VaR) question of longevity risk. The VaR framework presented here requires stochastic projection models.

Cairns (2011) warns of the risks in relying on a single model by posing the oft-overlooked questions "what if the parameters ... have been miscalibrated?" and "what if the model itself is wrong?" Cairns further writes that any solution "should be applicable to a wide range of stochastic mortality models." The framework described below works with a wide variety of models, enabling practitioners to explore the impact of model risk on capital requirements.

Data

The data used in this chapter are the all-cause number of deaths at age x last birthday during each calendar year y, split by gender. Corresponding midyear population estimates are also given.

The data therefore lend themselves to modeling the force of mortality, $\mu_{x + 1/2,\, y + 1/2}$, without further adjustment. We use data provided by the Office for National Statistics (ONS) for England and Wales for the calendar years 1961–2010 inclusive. This particular data set has death counts and estimated exposures at individual ages up to age 104. We will work here with the subset of ages 50–104, which is most relevant for the insurance products sold at around retirement ages. The deaths and exposures in the age group labeled "105+" were not used. More detailed discussion of this data set, particularly regarding the estimated exposures, can be found in Richards (2008). Note that the ONS has subsequently revised the population estimates for 2002–10.

One consequence of only having data to age 104 is that one has to decide how to calculate annuity factors for comparison. One option would be to create an arbitrary extension of the projected mortality rates up to (say) age 120. Another alternative is simply to look at temporary annuities to avoid artefacts arising from the arbitrary extrapolation. We use the latter approach here, and we therefore calculate continuously paid temporary annuity factors. Restricting our calculations to temporary annuities has no meaningful consequences at the main ages of interest, as shown by the examples in Richards *et al.* (forthcoming). Although we have opted for the temporary annuity solution, it is worth noting that the models of Currie *et al.* (2004) and Cairns *et al.* (2006) are capable of simultaneously extrapolating mortality rates to higher (and lower) ages at the same time as projecting forward in time. These models therefore deserve a special place in the actuarial toolkit, and the subject is discussed in more detail by Richards and Currie (2011) and Currie (2011).

In this chapter we are concerned only with longevity trend risk. However, there are other aspects of longevity risk that an insurer or pension scheme needs to take into account, and an overview of these is given in Richards *et al.* (forthcoming).

A Value-at-Risk Framework

This section describes a one-year framework for longevity risk based on the sensitivity of the central projection to new data. This approach differs from the models of Börger (2010) and Plat (2011), which seek to model the trend and its tail distribution directly. Those authors also present specific models, whereas the framework described here is general and can accommodate a wide range of stochastic projection models. In contrast to Plat (2011), who modeled longevity risk and insurance risk, the framework here is intended to focus solely on longevity trend risk in pensions and annuities in payment.

At a high level we use a stochastic model to simulate the mortality experience of an extra year, and then feed this into an updated model to see how the central projection is affected. This is repeated many times to generate a probability distribution of how the central projection might change over a one-year time horizon. In more detail the framework is as follows.

1. First, select a data set covering ages x_L to x_H and running from years y_L to y_H. This includes the deaths at each age in each year, d_{xy}, and the corresponding population exposures. The population exposures can be either the initial exposed-to-risk, E_{xy}, or the midyear central exposed-to-risk, E^c_{xy}. For this process we need the exposures for the start of year y_{H+1}, so, if the basic exposures are central, we will approximate the initial exposures using $E_{x,y_{H+1}} \approx E^c_{x-1,y_H} - d_{x-1,y_H} \div 2$.

2. Next, select a statistical model and fit it to the data set in step 1. This gives fitted values for log μ_{xy}, where x is the age in years and y is the calendar year. We can use the projections from this model to calculate various life expectancies and annuity factors at specimen ages if desired.

3. Use the statistical model in step 2 to generate sample paths for log $\mu_{x,y_{H+1}}$, i.e. for the year immediately following the last year for which we have data. These sample paths can include trend uncertainty or volatility or both. In practice, the dominant source of uncertainty over a one-year horizon is usually volatility, so this should always be included. We can estimate $q_{x,y_{H+1}}$, the binomial probability of death in year y_{H+1}, by using the approximation $q \approx 1 - e^{-\mu}$.

4. We simulate the number of deaths in year y_{H+1} at each age as a binomial random variable. The population counts are the $E_{x,y_{H+1}}$ from step 1, and the binomial probabilities are those simulated in step 3. This gives us simulated death counts at each age apart from x_L, and we can calculate corresponding midyear exposures as $E^c_{x,y_{H+1}} \approx E_{x,y_{H+1}} - d_{x,y_{H+1}} \div 2$.

5. We then temporarily append our simulated data from step 4 to the real data in step 1, creating a single simulation of the data we might have in one year's time. The missing data for age x_L in year y_{H+1} is treated

by providing dummy values and assigning a weight of zero. We then refit the statistical model to this combined data set, reperform the projections, and recalculate the life expectancies and annuity values at the specimen ages using the updated central projection.

6. Repeat steps 3 to 5 n times, where n might be at least 1,000 (say) for Solvency II-style work. It is implicit in this methodology that there is no migration, or that if there is migration its net effect is zero, i.e. that immigrants have similar numbers and mortality characteristics to emigrants. The choice of n will have a number of practical considerations, but for estimating the 99.5th percentile a minimum value of $n = 1,000$ is required.

Figure 1 shows the resulting updated central projections from a handful of instances of performing steps 1-6. Note that we do not require nested simulations, as the central projection is evaluated without the need to perform any simulations. The nature of projections and their standard errors is discussed in more detail in Richards *et al.* (forthcoming).

Figure 1. One-year approach to longevity risk. Experience data for 2011 are simulated using sample paths from an ARIMA(3,1,3) process and the Lee–Carter (1992) model is refitted each time the 2011 data are simulated. The changes in central projections give an idea of how the best estimate could change over the course of a year based on new data. Although we are interested in the one-year change in annuity factor, we have to do a full multiyear projection to calculate the annuity factor.

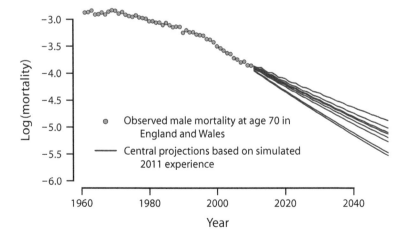

After following this procedure we have a set, S, of n realized values of how life expectancies or annuity values can change based on the addition of a single year's data:

$$S = \{\bar{a}^j_x; j = 1, 2, ..., n\} \tag{1}$$

S can then be used to set a capital requirement to cover potential changes in expectation of longevity trend risk over one year. For example, a one-year VaR estimate of trend-risk capital would be:

$$(99.5\text{th percentile of } S \div \text{Mean of } S - 1) \times 100\% \tag{2}$$

Readers interested in the technical details of how percentiles are estimated from sets of data in this chapter, which models to use, or how to generate sample paths can consult Richards et al. (forthcoming).

Results of the One-Year VaR Approach

The framework described in the previous section is applied to selected models and the results are shown in Table 1.

Table 1. Average and 99.5th percentile values for temporary annuity factor, $\bar{a}^{3\%}_{70:\overline{35}|}$, from 2011 using models of male mortality applied to data from England and Wales, 1961–2010, ages 50–104. Temporary annuities to age 105 are used to avoid distortions caused by extrapolation to higher ages. Discounting is at 3% per annum. Results are based on 1,000 simulations according to the procedure described in steps 1–6 of the text.

Model	Value of $\bar{a}^{3\%}_{70:\overline{35}|}$		Capital requirement, $((b) \div (a) - 1) \times 100\%$
	(a) average value	(b) 99.5th percentile	
Lee and Carter (1992)	12.14	12.72	4.80%
Cairns et al. (2006)	11.98	12.44	3.85%
Age-period-cohort (Currie, 2012)	12.61	13.04	3.40%
2D age-period (Currie et al., 2004)	12.80	13.69	6.97%

One issue with the figures in Table 1 is that they are sample quantiles, i.e. they are based on the top few order statistics and are therefore themselves random variables with uncertainty surrounding their estimated value. One approach is to use a more sophisticated estimator of the quantile, such as that from Harrell and Davis (1982). Such estimators are not only more efficient, but they also produce standard errors for the estimator without any distributional assumptions.

Figure 2 shows the Harrell–Davis estimates of the VaR capital for a smoothed version of the Lee–Carter model, together with a confidence envelope around those estimates.

Figure 2. Harrell–Davis (1982) estimate of the 99.5% VaR capital requirement for a smoothed version of the Lee–Carter model in Table 1, together with an approximate 95% confidence envelope.

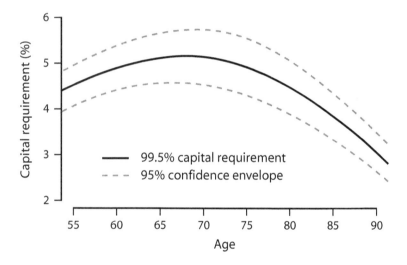

Benchmarking VaR Capital Requirements

The approach in this chapter is documented in Richards *et al.* (forthcoming), a paper that was presented to actuaries in Edinburgh and London in November 2012. One of the topics which came up during the discussion was how the answers from the VaR method squared with how life offices actually change their projection bases in practice. In particular, some commentators were interested in what might be regarded as a "real world" example of a sudden change in projection basis, and how this might compare with the results given by the VaR framework.

As it happens, we do have a historical example to call on, and furthermore it is recent enough to be directly relevant. At the end of the last millennium, Willets (1999) brought the cohort effect to the attention of the UK actuarial profession, a study that was later followed up by Willets (2004). The former paper was such an important piece of work that the projections in CMI (2002) were released as a stop-gap replacement for the projections in CMI (1999). The change in projections was large enough for one UK life office to make a stock exchange announcement because of the increase in its annuity reserves. This is exactly the sort of "real world" example of a change in mortality projections that we are looking for, and one unconnected with the VaR framework or any stochastic model. We can therefore use this change from CMI (1999) to the so-called cohort projections as a benchmark example of a sudden change in trend expectation, based on new information.

Under the then-outgoing CMI (1999) projection, the annuity factor at age 70 was 10.89.[1] Using the replacement short-cohort projection, the same annuity factor became 11.28, a 3.60% increase. Using the more commonly used medium-cohort projection, the annuity factor became 11.35, a 4.20% increase. Life offices switching from the CMI (1999) projection to one of the new cohort projections would therefore have experienced a relatively sudden increase in capital requirement in line with the sort of figures produced by the VaR framework in Table 1. In practice, a life office would often stage the basis transition over a few years, but it would know at the outset the size of the change it was aiming for.

Of course, modern economic conditions are different from a decade ago, and we know that the trend-risk capital depends on the yield curve. Indeed, with lower discount rates the sensitivity of annuity reserves to mortality changes has increased. Nevertheless, the historical example of the switch from CMI (1999) to the cohort projections provides a broad corroboration of the one-year VaR capital figures cited here and in Richards et al. (forthcoming).

Conclusions

Longevity risk has a number of components, of which trend risk is just one. The longevity trend risk faced by insurers and defined-benefit pension schemes exists as a long-term accumulation of small changes, which could together add up to an adverse trend. Despite the long-term nature of longevity risk, there are reasons why insurers and others want to look at longevity through a one-year, value-at-risk prism. These reasons include the one-year horizon demanded by the ICA regime in the United Kingdom and the pending Solvency II regime for the European Union.

This chapter has described a framework for putting a long-term longevity trend risk into a one-year view for setting capital requirements. The results of using this framework are consistent with a recent historical example of a sudden change in expectations.

Whatever the choice of method—stressed trend, mortality shock, or value-at-risk—the actual capital requirements depend on the age and interest rate used in the calculations, and also the choice of model. However, the approaches used in this chapter suggest that the capital requirement in respect of longevity trend risk in level annuities should not be less than 3½% of the best-estimate reserve, and will often be higher. For escalating annuities, or for indexed pensions in payment, the minimum capital requirement in respect of longevity trend risk will be higher still.

More Info

Articles:

Börger, Matthias. "Deterministic shock vs. stochastic value-at-risk: An analysis of the Solvency II standard model approach to longevity risk." *Blätter der DGVFM* 31:2 (October 2010): 225–259. Online at: dx.doi.org/10.1007/s11857-010-0125-z

Cairns, Andrew J. G. "Modelling and management of longevity risk: Approximations to survival functions and dynamic hedging." *Insurance: Mathematics and Economics* 49:3 (November 2011): 438–453. Online at: www.ma.hw.ac.uk/~andrewc/papers/ajgc62.pdf

Cairns, Andrew J. G., David Blake, and Kevin Dowd. "A two-factor model for stochastic mortality with parameter uncertainty: Theory and calibration." *Journal of Risk and Insurance* 73:4 (December 2006): 687–718. Online at: dx.doi.org/10.1111/j.1539-6975.2006.00195.x

Currie, Iain D. "Modelling and forecasting the mortality of the very old." *ASTIN Bulletin* 41:2 (2011): 419–427. Online at: www.ma.hw.ac.uk/~iain/research/Astin_2011_419_427.pdf

Currie, Iain D. "Forecasting with the age-period-cohort model?" *Proceedings of 27th International Workshop on Statistical Modelling,* Prague, July 16–22, 2012; pp. 87–92. Online at: www.ma.hw.ac.uk/~iain/research/prague.pdf

Currie, Iain D., Maria Durban, and Paul H. C. Eilers. "Smoothing and forecasting mortality rates." *Statistical Modelling* 4:4 (December 2004): 279–298. Online at: dx.doi.org/10.1191/1471082X04st080oa

Harrell, Frank E., and C. E. Davis. "A new distribution-free quantile estimator." *Biometrika* 69:3 (December 1982): 635–640. Online at: dx.doi.org/10.1093/biomet/69.3.635

Lee, Ronald D., and Lawrence Carter. "Modeling and forecasting U.S. mortality." *Journal of the American Statistical Association* 87:419 (September 1992): 659–671. Online at: tinyurl.com/l2uq98g [PDF].

Plat, Richard. "One-year value-at-risk for longevity and mortality." *Insurance: Mathematics and Economics* 49:3 (November 2011): 462–470. Online at: dx.doi.org/10.1016/j.insmatheco.2011.07.002

Richards, S. J. "Detecting year-of-birth mortality patterns with limited data." *Journal of the Royal Statistical Society, Series A* 171:1 (January 2008): 279–298. Online at: dx.doi.org/10.1111/j.1467-985X.2007.00501.x

Richards, S. J., and I. D. Currie. "Extrapolating mortality projections by age." *Life and Pension Risk* (June 2011): 34–38. Online at: www.richardsconsulting.co.uk/ExtrapolationByAge.pdf

Richards, S. J., I. D. Currie, and G. P. Ritchie. "A value-at-risk framework for longevity trend risk." *British Actuarial Journal* (forthcoming). Online at: dx.doi.org/10.1017/S1357321712000451

The Economist. "How innovation happens: The ferment of finance." In "Playing with fire," special report on financial innovation. February 25, 2012; p. 8. Online at: www.economist.com/node/21547998

Willets, Richard C. "The cohort effect: Insights and explanations." *British Actuarial Journal* 10:4 (October 2004): 833–877. Online at: dx.doi.org/10.1017/S1357321700002762

Reports:

Continuous Mortality Investigation (CMI) Bureau. "Continuous mortality investigation reports." No. 17. Institute of Actuaries and Faculty of Actuaries, July 1999. Online at: tinyurl.com/l7p7fgl

Continuous Mortality Investigation (CMI) Mortality Sub-Committee. "An interim basis for adjusting the '92' series mortality projections for cohort effects." Working paper no. 1. December 2002. Online at: tinyurl.com/lmj5wwd

European Commission, Internal Market and Services Directorate General. "QIS5 technical specifications: Annex to call for advice from CEIOPS on QIS5." July 5, 2010; p. 152.

Willets, Richard C. "Mortality in the next millennium." Staple Inn Actuarial Society (SIAS), December 7, 1999. Online at: www.sias.org.uk/view_paper?id=MortalityMillennium

---

1 Using 100% of PMA92 for a single-life annuity paid continuously to a male aged 70, starting in 1992 (PMA92, where PMA is "Pensioners, males, amounts," is the "92" series of mortality tables published by the Institute and Faculty of Actuaries). Annuity payments are discounted at 3% interest per annum.

The Financial Impact of Longevity Risk[1]

by S. Erik Oppers

This Chapter Covers
- The concept of longevity risk.
- Problems of forecasting longevity.
- Quantification of the longevity risk faced by pension providers.
- Ways to mitigate longevity risk through market-based transfer.
- The role of government in facilitating longevity risk mitigation in the private sector.

Introduction

Longevity risk is the risk that actual life spans of individuals or of whole populations will exceed expectations. People have been living longer lives for at least a century now, and this has obvious benefits. But governments, private companies, and individuals all potentially face financial risks if people on average live longer than expected. In particular, defined-benefit pension plans, insurance companies that offer life annuities, and governments that sponsor old-age social security systems would have to pay benefits for longer than anticipated, increasing the net present value of their liabilities. Individuals without a defined-benefit pension also face longevity risk, as they may run out of private pension savings if they live longer than expected.

The Difficulty of Forecasting Longevity

The main source of longevity risk is the discrepancy between expected and actual life spans, which has been large and one-sided: forecasters, regardless of the techniques they use, have consistently underestimated how long people will live. These forecast errors have been systematic over time and across populations. A study by the UK Office for National Statistics has evaluated the forecast errors made in the United Kingdom over the past decades (Figure 1). It showed that future estimates of longevity were consistently too low in each successive forecast, and errors were generally large (Shaw, 2007). In fact, underestimation is widespread across countries: 20-year forecasts of longevity made in recent decades in Australia, Canada, Japan, New Zealand, and the United States have been too low by an average of three years (Bongaarts and Bulatao, 2000). The systematic errors appear to arise from the assumption that currently observed rates of longevity improvement will slow down in the future (Box 1). In reality, they have not slowed down, partly because medical advances, such as better treatments for cancer and HIV, have continued to raise life expectancy.

The longevity risk resulting from these forecast errors is large and affects all of society. The International Monetary Fund (2012) calculated that if everyone in 2050 lived just three years longer than is now expected—three years being the average underestimation of longevity in the past—society would need extra resources equal to 1% to 2% of GDP per year. If this "longevity shock" occurred today and society wanted to save to pay for these extra resources for the next 40 years (that is, fully fund these additional "pension liabilities"), advanced countries would have to set aside around 50% of their 2010 GDP and emerging economies would need around 25% of 2010 GDP—a sum totaling tens of trillions of dollars. As such, longevity risk potentially adds one-half to the vast costs of aging up to the year 2050—and aging costs themselves are not fully recognized in most long-term fiscal plans.

Figure 1. Projected life expectancies at birth for males in the United Kingdom, 1966–2031, according to successive forecasts made between 1971 and 2010. Actual life expectancy up to 2011 included for comparison. (*Source*: UK Office of National Statistics.)

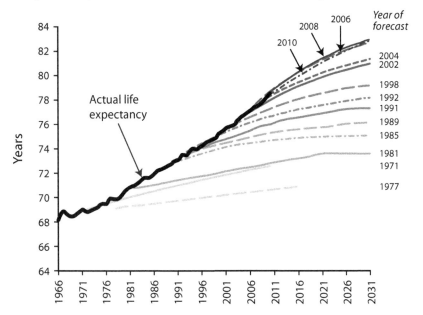

Box 1. Forecasting Longevity

Longevity forecasts can be made using various methods. Forecasting models can be broadly categorized into: methods that attempt to understand and use the underlying drivers of mortality (process-based methods and econometric models); and extrapolative methods, which use only historical trends to forecast future developments.

So-called process-based methods and econometric models seek an understanding of the underlying factors that drive death rates. These methods use biomedical assumptions to forecast death rates from various causes, leading to longevity rates for "cohorts" (people in a particular demographic section of the population born in a particular year or period). Econometric methods principally model longevity as a function of general economic, environmental, and epidemiological factors. A difficulty with both approaches is that they require a model for the relationship between underlying factors and longevity. Also, if they are used to make forecasts of longevity, forecasts need to be available for any underlying factors used in the model.

Extrapolative approaches do not attempt to identify the drivers of death rates but use only information contained in historical data to forecast future mortality rates. Such models could assume that historical trends continue going forward, either exactly or in some "smoothed" form, or could try to derive a more sophisticated model from historical trends (possibly disaggregated by cohort) that could then be used for a forecast. Methods can be deterministic—meaning that they directly calculate future changes from past trends—or stochastic, meaning that they apply random changes from a probability distribution derived from past developments to generate future changes. A drawback of the extrapolative approach is that it looks only at the past and does not use available information (or assumptions) about possible future developments that affect longevity, such as medical breakthroughs or changes in behavior.

The Effect of Longevity Risk on Pension Plans

Longevity risk also significantly affects corporate sponsors of retirement plans. The typical assumptions for pension liability valuations in many countries do not adequately account for expected future developments in longevity, exposing pension providers to significant longevity risk. Although valuations typically incorporate some future increases that exceed current life expectancy tables, those increases are still much smaller in a number of countries than those that have actually occurred in the past (Table 1).

Table 1. Pension estimates and population estimates of male life expectancy at age 65 in selected advanced economies (years)

	1. Typical assumption for pension liability valuation*	2. Population life expectancy†	Difference 1 – 2	Observed improvements since 1990‡
Australia	19.9	18.7	1.2	3.5
Austria	20.8	17.0	3.8	3.4
Canada	19.4	18.2	1.2	2.6
Germany	19.0	16.9	2.1	3.3
Ireland	21.0	16.7	4.3	3.8
Japan	18.8	18.6	0.2	2.7
United Kingdom	21.2	17.2	4.0	3.9
United States	18.4	17.5	0.9	2.4

* Takes into account some future improvement in longevity.
† Does not take into account future improvement in longevity.
‡ Difference between the latest population life expectancy at age 65 and that in 1990 (taken from the Human Mortality Database).
Sources: Sithole *et al.* (2012); Human Mortality Database as of February 22, 2012.

The regression analysis by Kisser *et al.* (2012) shows that a three-year increase in longevity would increase pension fund liabilities by 9% (Box 2). The estimated shock is considerable, since it affects a large stock of liabilities—multiples of sponsors' typical yearly contributions would be necessary to increase assets commensurately. For example, a longevity adjustment in the Netherlands in 2010 led to an increase in liabilities of the pension sector of about 7% (or 8% of GDP). This increase in liabilities could not be matched by an increase in assets through employer and employee contributions; other measures to cover the shortfall are now being considered, including foregoing indexation of pensions and a possible lowering of nominal pensions.

Box 2. Changing Longevity Assumptions by US Defined-Benefit Plans

The effect on corporate pensions can be illustrated by an example that uses detailed data from the US Department of Labor (DOL) to estimate the longevity risk faced by defined-benefit pension plans in the United States.[2] The DOL's Form 5500 contains important statistics for evaluating longevity risk for large US pension funds, including total liabilities, number of plan participants, and the actuarial assumptions used. Data are available for the period between 1995 and 2007 (the most current year published).

The Form 5500 data suggest that the use of outdated mortality tables has been a common practice (Table 2).[3] Until recently, a majority of plans used the Group Annuity Mortality Table (GAM) of 1983, and many still did at the end of the sample period, implying a lag of almost a quarter century in their mortality assumptions. Throughout the sample, only a few plans used the latest available table.[4] This exposes many pension providers to substantial longevity risk.

Table 2. Mortality tables used by reporting pension plans (%)

Year	1951 GAM	1971 IAM	1984 UP	1983 IAM	1983 GAM	1994 UP	2007 Mortality table	Other	Hybrid	None
1995	1	0	7	1	48	5	0	3	22	0
1996	0	0	6	0	57	1	0	6	19	0
1997	0	0	4	0	62	1	0	6	17	0
1998	0	0	4	0	65	1	0	6	15	0
1999	0	0	3	0	67	1	0	7	14	3
2000	0	0	3	0	68	2	0	7	13	2
2001	0	0	2	0	69	2	0	8	12	2
2002	0	0	2	0	69	2	0	10	11	3
2003	0	0	2	0	65	3	0	13	11	3
2004	0	0	1	0	63	3	0	17	10	3
2005	0	0	1	0	49	3	0	31	10	3
2006	0	0	1	0	28	3	0	55	8	3
2007	0	0	1	0	15	2	12	57	6	4

Note: GAM, Group Annuity Mortality Table; IAM, Individual Annuity Mortality Table; UP, Unisex Pension Table. "Other" includes undefined mortality tables. "Hybrid" means that the standard mortality tables have been modified by the pension fund. "None" means that no mortality table has been used.
Sources: US Department of Labor and IMF staff estimates.

Each mortality table implies different life expectancies of retirees, and pension plans see a realization of longevity risk when they shift to the use of an updated table. The difference in implied life expectancy of 63-year-old males (the average retirement age in the sample) between the most dated and the most current mortality table is 5.2 years (see Figure 2). For the substantial fraction of plans that previously employed the 1983 Group Annuity Mortality Table, a switch to the 2007 table (as required since 2008) implies an increase in longevity of 2.1 years.

Figure 2. Life expectancy at age 63 by year of mortality table (GAM, Group Annuity Mortality Table; IAM, Individual Annuity Mortality Table; UP, Unisex Pension Table). (*Sources*: see IMF, 2012.)

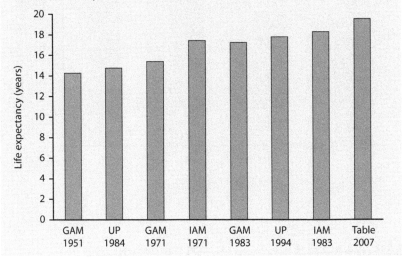

Longevity risk is exacerbated in the current low interest rate environment. The higher future liabilities arising from longevity risk are discounted less with lower interest rates. Calculations in IMF (2012) confirm that lower discount rates have significant effects on the size of longevity risk, as shown in Figure 3. With a discount rate of 6%, a three-year extension in average life expectancy increases liabilities by 8% in this example; with a discount rate of 2%, the same three-year shock increases liabilities by almost 14%. Low interest rates therefore affect pension plans in two ways: by increasing their liabilities, and by exposing them to higher longevity risk.

Figure 3. Increase in actuarial liabilities resulting from a three-year increase in longevity for different discount rates. (*Source*: IMF staff estimates. *Note*: Actuarial liabilities are projected benefit obligations of a model pension plan.)

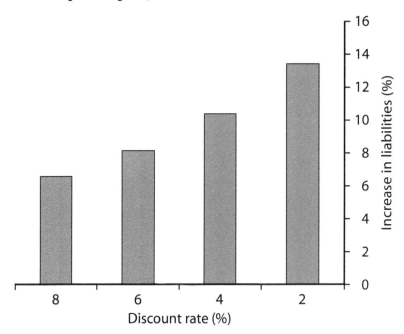

Mitigating Longevity Risk through Market-Based Transfer

Like any other risk faced by economic agents—such as interest rate or exchange rate risk—longevity risk should be recognized and addressed. For private pension providers, an effective way to address longevity risk is to "insure" against this risk. In recent years, a market has developed where the "supply" of longevity risk meets the "demand" for this risk, allowing those who hold it (including individuals, governments, and private providers of retirement income) to transfer longevity risk to (re-)insurers, capital market participants, and private companies that may be better placed to deal with it. They might be in this position because they would benefit from unexpected increases in longevity (providers of long-term care and health care, for example, or sellers of life insurance). In theory, in this market the price of longevity risk would adjust to a level at which the risk would be optimally spread among the market participants.

Simply designed, over-the-counter (OTC) bilateral contracts and longevity bonds are the two principal instruments through which longevity risk can be transferred. The bilateral solutions include pension buy-outs and buy-ins, swaps, and other derivative contracts.

Bilateral Contracts

Buy-ins and buy-outs are simple transactions that accomplish risk transfer, but each has different implications for the sponsor. In a buy-out transaction, all of the pension fund's assets and liabilities are transferred to an insurer for an up-front premium (Figure 4). The pension liabilities and their offsetting assets are removed from the pension fund sponsor's balance sheet and the insurer takes over full responsibility for making payments to pensioners. In a buy-in, the sponsor pays an up-front premium to the insurer, who then makes periodic payments to the pension fund sponsor equal to those made by the sponsor to its members. This "insurance policy" is held as an asset by the pension plan; the premium is the cost of the insurance policy that guarantees payments even if retirees live longer than expected.

Figure 4. Structure of pension buy-out and buy-in transactions

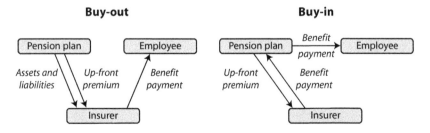

In another type of bilateral transaction, the longevity swap, the pension fund obtains a similar protection from higher than expected pension payouts. The plan sponsor makes periodic fixed "premium" payments to the swap counterparty, which in turn makes periodic payments that are based on the difference between the actual and expected benefit payments (Figure 5). The sponsor maintains full responsibility for making benefit payments to its employees. An advantage of buy-ins and swaps is that they can be used to hedge the longevity risk associated with specific subsets of the underlying population. An advantage of swaps is that longevity risk can be isolated, whereas buy-in and buy-out transactions typically also transfer the investment risk of the assets. Longevity swaps can also be combined with other types of derivative contract, such as inflation, interest rate, and total return swaps, to create so-called "synthetic" buy-ins that transfer all of the risks.

Figure 5. Structure of longevity swap transactions

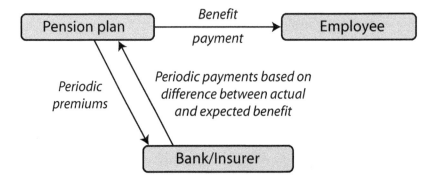

Longevity Bonds

The payout on a longevity bond would depend on an index that tracks the longevity experience of a given population (Figure 6). The periodic payment (or coupon) on a longevity bond would be proportional to the number of survivors in the population. Therefore, the issuer of the bond (an investment bank or insurance company) pays more to the owner of the bond (the pension fund sponsor) when longevity is higher. The owner of the bond could thus use the periodic payments from the bond to offset any higher than expected payments to retirees. The offset is likely not to be perfect because of basis risk, which exists because the payout is typically linked to an index that is based on the longevity experience of a sample population, whereas actual payouts depend on the actual pool of retirees of the pension provider.

Figure 6. Structure of longevity bond transactions

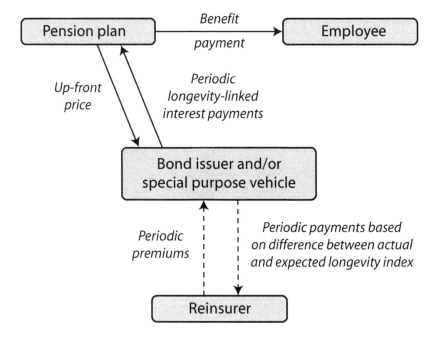

Obstacles to Market Development

The use of capital market-based longevity risk management solutions has been growing, but their use remains small, with the notable exception of the swap, buy-in, and buy-out markets in the United Kingdom and the Netherlands (Figure 7). Explanations for the slow growth include a lack of recognition among pension plan sponsors of the importance of longevity risk (Figue 8), a lack of familiarity of the market with longevity risk transfer, the basis risk inherent in most risk transfer instruments, counterparty risk (exacerbated by the long duration of longevity risk and its mitigation instruments), a lack of reliable and sufficiently detailed information about longevity developments, and a dearth of "natural buyers" of longevity risk compared to the potential sellers. While life insurers have a natural hedge against longevity risk, their life exposure is dwarfed by the global exposure to longevity risk.

Figure 7. Longevity risk transfers in the United Kingdom by type of transfer. (*Sources*: Hymans Robertson LLP, London, and IMF staff estimates.)

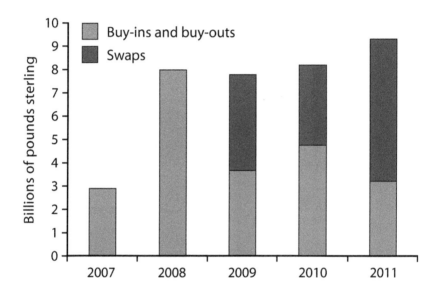

Figure 8. Attitudes of pension plan sponsors toward hedging pension risk. (*Source*: Aon Hewitt's "Global pension risk survey 2011: European findings.")

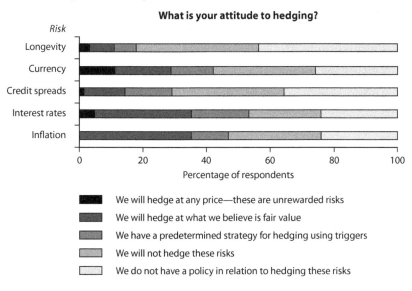

Summary and Further Steps

The size of longevity risk on a global scale is vast. The IMF (2012) showed that if everyone in 2050 lives just three years longer than is now projected—which has been the average underestimation of longevity in the past—the already very large costs of aging could increase by some 50%. This is equivalent to trillions of dollars.

Governments in particular already bear a significant amount of longevity risk. Their longevity exposure is threefold: through public pension plans, through social security schemes, and as the "holder of last resort" of longevity risk of individuals and financial institutions. If individuals run out of resources in retirement, they will need to depend on social security schemes to provide minimum standards of living. There may also be an expectation that governments will step in if financial institutions or corporations face threats to their solvency from longevity exposure.

Individuals bear significant longevity risk if they lack pension plans that guarantee an income for life, but they also have a powerful tool to offset this risk: their labor income. One of the most effective ways to meet the increasing costs of aging and to offset longevity risk is to delay retirement. A longer working life benefits all sectors: the government collects more labor taxes, pension plans receive more contributions, and individuals themselves can increase their financial buffers.

Providers of guaranteed retirement income in the private sector also face considerable longevity risk, the mitigation of which could be achieved in part through market-based transfer. This market has, however, been slow to take off for a number of reasons.

Further Steps: The Role of Government

Government may be able to facilitate the private sector in further development of an efficient market for longevity risk transfer through a number of measures, including:

- *Provision of more-detailed longevity data*: The lack of detailed longevity and related demographic data is a major constraint facing the longevity risk market. Governments are best placed to provide such data, perhaps through national statistical offices or government actuaries. Essential data would include longevity information that is disaggregated by geographic area, as well as by gender, socioeconomic status, cause of death, and occupation.

- *Enhancing regulation and supervision*: Governments could provide tighter regulation to promote the recognition and mitigation of longevity risk, including through stricter funding requirements and enhanced accounting transparency for pension funds and insurance companies. Indeed, in jurisdictions where longevity risk is currently not covered in pension regulations it should be included.

- *Improving the education of market participants*: Surveys suggest that market participants are generally insufficiently aware of longevity risk, and that there is a role for government to promote awareness of the importance of addressing longevity risk as has been done for other financial risks.

Better recognition and mitigation of longevity risk should be undertaken now, including through risk sharing between individuals, pension providers, and the public sector, and through the development of a liquid longevity risk transfer market. Longevity risk is already on the doorstep, and addressing it effectively will become more difficult the longer remedial action is delayed.

More Info

Books:
Bongaarts, John, and Rodolfo A. Bulatao (eds). *Beyond Six Billion: Forecasting the World's Population*. Washington, DC: National Academy Press, 2000.

International Monetary Fund. "The financial impact of longevity risk." In *Global Financial Stability Report: The Quest for Lasting Stability*. Washington, DC: IMF, 2012; ch. 4. Online at: www.imf.org/external/pubs/ft/gfsr/2012/01/pdf/text.pdf

Articles:
Shaw, Chris. "Fifty years of United Kingdom national population projections: How accurate have they been?" *Population Trends* 128 (Summer 2007): 8–23. Online at: tinyurl.com/kph7me7 [PDF].

Sithole, T. Z., S. Haberman, and R. J. Verrall. "Second international comparative study of mortality tables for pension fund retirees." *British Actuarial Journal* 17:3 (September 2012): 650–671. Online at: dx.doi.org/10.1017/S1357321712000207

Report:
Kisser, Michael, John Kiff, Erik S. Oppers, and Mauricio Soto. "The impact of longevity improvements on U.S. corporate defined benefit pension plans." Working paper no. 12/170. IMF, June 2012. Online at: www.imf.org/external/pubs/ft/wp/2012/wp12170.pdf

Website:
The Human Mortality Database (detailed population and mortality data for 37 countries): www.mortality.org

1 This chapter is adapted from International Monetary Fund (2012). The views expressed herein are those of the author and should not be attributed to the IMF, its executive board, or its management.

2 This analysis is taken from Kisser *et al.* (2012).

3 Actuaries typically use mortality statistics to compute liabilities. Mortality is of course the complement of longevity, and therefore conceptually equivalent.

4 For some pension funds, information on the underlying mortality table is not available as the corresponding tables are classified as "other" with no further information given. Anecdotal evidence suggests that some funds may have switched to another recently proposed table (the RP-2000 mortality table).

How Should Insurers Optimally Manage Market Risk?

by Patrick O. J. Kelliher

This Chapter Covers
- What is market risk?
- Market risk in different companies and countries.
- Market risk governance and policy.
- How market risk is identified.
- Modeling and measuring market risk.
- Appetite for market risk.
- Monitoring market risk.
- Management of market risk.

Introduction

Market risk is a key risk for most life insurers, many of whom need to manage guarantees on volatile portfolios of assets. For general insurers, the importance of market risk varies depending on the tail of the business, but investment income is a key driver of profitability and market risk encompasses variations in this income. The author's experience is of the life insurance market in the United Kingdom, and there is a bias in coverage toward this market, but it is hoped that the points made are applicable to other insurers.

What Is Market Risk?

Any framework for market risk should start from clear definitions of market risks as part of a comprehensive risk universe. There is no definitive classification of market risks *per se*—each company will use one that suits its needs, but the market risk classification should be suitably granular to address the many different types of risks. It should also identify areas of overlap with other risks, not least as there may be separate accountabilities for these within a firm. The actuarial profession in the United Kingdom has published a paper on risk classification (Kelliher *et al.*, 2011), together with a spreadsheet of detailed risk categories, which may be of use in this regard.[1] This defines market risk as "the risk that as a result of market movements, a firm may be exposed to fluctuations in the value of its assets, the amount of its liabilities, or the income from its assets," and then identifies 11 high-level categories and nearly 100 subcategories of market risk.

Market Risk in Different Companies and Countries

There are wide divergences between the market risk exposures of insurers in different countries. In the United Kingdom, life insurers have exposure to guarantees under "with-profits" policies, where part of the assets is invested in equities, effectively giving rise to an exotic put option position. Unit-linked funds offered by life insurers are a key investment vehicle for pensions. These generally contain no guarantees, with market risk borne by the policyholder, but the life insurer is exposed to fluctuations in fund-related fees. Until recently, pension funds have had to be converted into an annuity for life, and UK life insurers have substantial liabilities to this type of business, typically backed by corporate bonds to avail themselves of the liquidity premium on these (there being little need for liquidity as the annuities cannot be encashed), but this gives rise to exposure to movements in credit spreads.

By contrast, in the United States, with-profits or participatory business has evolved differently than in the United Kingdom, in part because of guaranteed surrender value requirements imposed by US regulators. Market risk exposure relates more to corporate bonds than to equities. Mutual funds rather than insurer unit-linked funds are the key vehicle for pension saving. Life insurer unit-linked offerings typically come as "variable annuities" with guarantees which are dynamically hedged. Conversion to an annuity for life is not mandatory, so this business is not as important as it is in the United Kingdom.

If we were to look at life insurance markets in the European Union and elsewhere, we would find further diversity—what is notable about market risk in life insurance is its heterogeneity between different countries.

There are further differences in the case of general insurers, which typically have a more short-term investment outlook, although certain long-tail lines of business may have a similar time-frame of investment to that of life insurers. Typically, assets held will be mainly cash and bonds, reflecting the nature of the liabilities, but some general insurers invest in equities and other risky assets to boost investment returns and profits. Indeed, one of the most famous equity investors, Warren Buffet's Berkshire Hathaway, is primarily a property and casualty insurer.

As well as market risks relating to policy liabilities, insurers may be exposed to market risk in respect of staff pension schemes. The accounting and regulatory capital treatment of staff pension schemes may vary, but the economic risk posed by such schemes should be captured in the market risk framework. Similarly, there is an economic value associated with the value in-force (VIF) of future fund-related charges, and while this may not be reflected in accounts or regulatory capital, the market risk framework should capture fluctuations in VIF due to market risks.

Market Risk Governance and Policy

The insurance company's board is ultimately responsible for ensuring that risks are properly managed and for putting the risk management framework in place. The board should approve the market risk policy that dictates how market risk should be managed. In the United Kingdom, the insurer's market risk policy should comply with the Financial Services Authority's *Prudential Sourcebook* guidelines, which are actually quite sensible in outlining what market risk policy should cover.[2]

The market risk policy may encompass derivative risks (if these are permitted), setting down limits on how derivatives are to be used as well as minimum requirements for derivative risk management. Alternatively there may be a separate, yet associated, derivative risk policy that encompasses not just market risks associated with derivatives but also counterparty and operational risks.

Market risk will generally be managed according to the "three lines of defence" model, with business units accepting primary responsibility for managing the risk as the first line, an independent risk management function forming the second line providing review and challenge on market risk, and internal audit providing assurance on market risk controls as part of the third line.

Most insurers will devolve the management of assets to fund managers who may or may not be part of the same financial group. Either way, while the task of managing assets and the risks associated with these is devolved, the responsibility for managing market risk remains with the insurer.

Market risk policy requirements should be embedded in investment management agreements (IMAs) with the fund manager. The life insurer should have an investment oversight committee to monitor whether the fund manager is adhering to the IMA as well as to monitor the manager's investment performance.

Identification of Market Risk

Based on the insurer's market risk classification system, the insurer should maintain a register of the market risks it faces. This should be reviewed at least annually to ensure that all market risks faced are captured. It should also be continuously updated as new risks are identified.

New risks may emerge due to new insurance product offerings, investment in new asset classes, use of new derivative instruments, and/or changes in the nature of existing asset classes. New product offerings should be subject to risk assessments that include market and other risks. As well as seeking to identify new market risks associated with the product, these assessments should also consider how well current models of market risk address existing risks associated with the new product.

A similar assessment process should be in place for new asset classes and derivative instruments. Whether an asset is truly "new" can be subjective, particularly for bonds where there is frequent innovation in terms of collateral, structure, etc. Fund managers may not consider an asset as new, but such judgments should be reviewed as part of the fund manager oversight process. The new asset class/derivative instrument assessment process should consider whether existing market risk models can be extended to cover the new asset or instrument, or whether a completely new model is required.

Insurers also need to be aware of changes in the nature of existing assets held. Again, bonds may be a problematic area, for example due to subtle changes in the quality of collateral offered on different issues.[3] Collateral may also vary under derivatives. This overlaps with credit risk, and there is a case for having a credit risk/counterparty risk committee regularly review bond holdings to pick up on such changes.

Insurers should carry out regular stress and scenario testing which may highlight market (and other) risks that have not previously been considered. They should also have a process to try to identify emerging risks, for example by holding regular workshops where participants are encouraged to think "outside the box."

Market Risk Modeling and Measurement

Having identified a risk, the next stage is to try to model it. There is often a wide range of techniques, statistical distributions, and data sets that can be used to model market risks. Whichever is chosen, it is important to illustrate the sensitivity of the result to alternative models, data, and assumptions so that senior management understand the weaknesses and limitations of the model.

Solvency II holds out the promise that an insurer's own model of market risk could form the basis for setting regulatory capital under the "internal model" approach. One of the requirements for this is the "use test," which requires that the internal model should be widely used across the business. Ideally, it should form the "house view" of that particular risk, being the default for modeling that risk for pricing, risk management, or other purposes. There will be some purposes for which an internal model is not suitable, but the reasons for this should be fed back into model development.

Another requirement for internal model approval—and good practice in any case—is that the model should be independently validated by a separate function. For example, the second-line risk management function might validate models proposed by the first-line actuarial function. Validation should consider qualitative aspects as well as quantitative techniques, such as back-testing.

It is important to note that there is no perfect model. Risks change over time and insurers should have a continuous cycle of model validation and improvement to ensure that models remain a reasonable approximation to reality.

Once we have models of market risks, we can measure these risks. There are many ways of doing this. At the heart of Solvency II is a "value-at-risk" (VaR) approach, which looks to ensure that we have enough economic capital to withstand risks over a one-year period at a 99.5% confidence level. By contrast, US regulatory capital requirements are based on a "conditional tail expectation" approach, which looks at the expected losses arising from a risk above a certain confidence level.

These capital figures can serve as risk measures: for example, the insurer may measure market risks as the one-year 99.5% VaR figures calculated for Solvency II. Alternatively, we may use a lower confidence level—for instance, 95% one-year VaR—as a measure, focusing on less extreme, more likely events that may occur.

Using internal models to measure market risk helps to satisfy the use test, but we could use other metrics either in addition to or in place of figures from internal models. For instance, we may have a measure of corporate bond spread risk based on the sensitivity of the corporate bond portfolio to a one basis point increase in spread. Whatever measure is chosen, the insurer should be able to update risk measures regularly in line with market conditions, using approximations if necessary.

Risk Appetite

Being able to measure a market risk helps a firm to determine its appetite for that risk; few if any firms will have an appetite for unquantifiable risks.

At the heart of any risk appetite framework is the concept of economic profit and whether rewards offset the risks involved. However, this is generally assessed at an aggregate level, allowing for diversification between market and other risks. Assessment should be supplemented by a separate consideration of risks on an undiversified basis, as market risks which may make a marginal contribution to diversified requirements may be significant on a stand-alone basis.

Undiversified Solvency II or other economic capital figures could be used as the basis for this assessment. Furthermore, projections of undiversified requirements as part of business planning could help serve as a basis for setting limits based on measures of undiversified requirements.

For example, the projected requirement at the end of the business planning period plus a margin could form the basis of a draft limit. This reflects the trajectory of undiversified market risk exposure that is implicit in the business plan. When this is presented to the board, it is made aware of the impact of the business plan on exposure to market risk, and it has the opportunity to amend the plan if it is not comfortable with the consequences. Quantitative limits on market risks can be set iteratively. Note that current exposures may be in excess of the board's long-term desired level. The board may set a tolerance for this excess exposure, accepting it in the short term, but indicating its desire to eliminate excess exposure over the medium term.

As well as quantitative risk appetite limits, the market risk appetite assessment process should also seek to elicit the board's view of individual risks in the form of appetite statements. This process should consider qualitative aspects, such as whether the insurer considers it has a core competence in managing a market risk, or whether it considers the risk to be adequately rewarded. For example, Berkshire Hathaway is a company which believes that it has a core competence in managing market risk, while many insurers would consider interest rate mismatches to be unrewarded as these can be readily addressed by matching cash flows and using swap overlays.

Below quantitative limits and qualitative statements, there will be lower-level requirements that should be codified in a market risk policy. For example, equity risk models typically assume a well-diversified portfolio, but a policy will need to stipulate tolerances for how (un)diversified a portfolio may be, particularly when some stocks may account for more than 5% of an index.[4]

Finally, risk appetite assessment needs to consider not just economic impacts but also the regulatory capital impacts of risk, and the impact of these on distributable cash flow. This will typically be assessed at an aggregate level across all risks, but market risks will influence the capital buffer that a firm needs to hold to keep the possibility of breaching regulatory requirements to an acceptable level.

Monitoring Market Risk

Having determined the means to measure and set appetite limits for risk, the next stage is to monitor risks to ensure that exposure remains within appetite, to assess the impact of market risks crystallizing, to identify new risks and issues emerging, and to refine the model of market risk and hence the "house view" of that risk.

If risk appetite limits are based on capital figures, ongoing estimates of these for capital management could also be used to see if exposures are within limits. Otherwise the measures on which limits are based will need to be reassessed regularly to ensure that the insurer stays within appetite.

This exposure monitoring process should be supplemented with key risk indicators (KRIs), which may serve as a proxy for market risk exposure and impacts. For instance, annuity liabilities may serve as a quantum of the market risk implicit in an annuity portfolio, while the S&P 500 Index level may serve as an indicator of the impact to date of US equity market movements.

It may be an idea to consider relative valuation-based metrics, such as rental yields and price–earnings ratios (PERs), as KRIs which may warn of market bubbles and hence a greater risk of a fall. For instance, the average UK PER since 1988 has been 17, with a standard deviation of 4.[5] A PER of 25 (i.e. two standard deviations above average) may flag possible overheating of equity markets, while a PER of 9 may indicate an undervalued market, and hedging out—and thus locking in—at this level may not be wise.

As well as quantitative limit monitoring, there needs to be a robust compliance process to ensure that fund managers are adhering to investment management agreements and that market risk policy is being adhered to across the organization. A sophisticated internal model and limit structure will count for nought if excessive concentrations in individual stocks and/or sectors are allowed to develop.

Managing Market Risk

Insurers will often have access to well-developed markets to hedge most market risks, or they may be able to match cash flows to minimize market risk. However, it is worth noting the following limitations.

- Equity risk exposure can be hedged using futures and options. However, the latter requires an up-front premium, while the latter has a hidden cost in that it typically locks in equity-related growth to the risk-free rate, foregoing any equity risk premium. This may have adverse reporting consequences if operating profits include this premium.

- Hedging using index derivatives gives rise to basis risk related to the tracking error between actual portfolio and index performance. On an unhedged basis, this basis risk may be diversified away against broader market risk, but it can be quite significant on a hedged basis.

- Equity basis risk will also arise between benchmark indices (like the FTSE All Share in the United Kingdom) and indices on which hedges are based (with the FTSE 100 being the most common in the United Kingdom).

- Basis risk also arises between credit default swap (CDS) premiums and spreads on bonds, and the current financial crisis has seen spreads on the latter rising faster than CDS premiums; this leads to greater falls in bonds than the rise in offsetting CDS positions, although to the extent that this relates to a greater liquidity premium there may be offsetting benefits in liability valuation.

- In hedging currency risk, if we are hedging a "risk-free" asset like US Treasury bonds, the hedge should compensate for movements in overseas yields as well as currency movements. However, if we hedge a corporate bond with a variable spread over risk-free, residual overseas interest rate risk will arise, while changing spreads can lead to under-/overhedging, resulting in quite a volatile combination of asset and hedge, which needs to be closely monitored.

- Dynamic hedging of options and guarantees will break down when markets move faster than the insurer can rebalance positions, as on "Black Monday," October 19, 1987. Ultimately, dynamic hedging can only mitigate, not eliminate, market risk exposures.

Finally, hedging using derivatives poses operational challenges in terms of: documentation, particularly for over-the-counter transactions; monitoring and rebalancing hedges; and valuing positions and managing collateral. Margin and collateral calls give rise to liquidity risk, which needs to be managed. Any program to hedge or otherwise manage market risk needs to have regard to the operational capabilities of the insurer and its fund manager.

Case Study: Interest Rate Risk

Here we will take the main points considered in this article and apply them to interest rate risk (defined here in terms of nominal rates and excluding risk relating to real yields on index-linked bonds and swaps).

Risk Definition

Interest rate risk is typically defined in terms of movements in risk-free rates, but what are these—the yields on government bonds, or swap rates? Whichever is chosen should be communicated to all involved in interest rate risk management to ensure that there is no ambiguity.

There is a residual risk relating to differences between government bond yields and swap rates which may be considered under interest rate risk or as a separate risk category in its own right. (It may be considered as the spread over or under swaps of sovereign bonds.)

Risk Identification

As an example, as part of the new product risk assessment of a variable annuity offering, a life insurer may identify a risk relating to the sensitivity of guarantee costs to interest rates (known as "rho"). This will be typically be hedged dynamically, but there may be exposure to interest rate changes between rebalancing. Given the short-term nature of exposure, existing models of interest rate risk looking at a one-year perspective may not be suitable.

Scenario analysis may generate scenarios that affect interest rates, and the insurer should consider what it may do to mitigate such changes. The scenarios should also be fed into interest rate risk models to see whether they invalidate these models—though this should be a two-way process as models could highlight unrealistic impacts under the scenario.

Risk Modeling

Modeling nominal interest rate risks is complicated by the need to model separate yet correlated changes at different points of the yield curve. A common approach to modeling the different parts of the curve is to use principal components analysis (PCA). This decomposes the variance–covariance matrix of rates at different terms into uncorrelated components, which generally turn out to be changes in the level, slope, and shape of the yield curve. Separate stresses for changes in the slope and shape of the yield curve can highlight mismatches at particular durations of the curve and exposure to nonparallel yield curve shifts, even if the portfolio is matched by duration.

Risk Measurement

The impact of PCA stresses at a 99.5% or 95% one-year level could be used as a risk metric. Another possible metric may be the "PV01," or the change in present value of assets and liabilities with a 1 bp change in yields. This will be linked to the duration of assets and liabilities. Ideally, risk measures would capture exposure to nonparallel as well as parallel yield curve movements.

Risk Appetite

Interest rate risk is often considered as unrewarded risk as it can typically be hedged by matching cash flows. However, matching may not be possible for long-term cash flows, while matching on an economic basis may lead to a mismatch on a regulatory capital basis and vice versa due to margins (e.g. for life expectancy) in the latter.

The insurer may also permit a degree of investment freedom to bond fund managers to benefit from their skills but at the expense of modest divergences from a matched position. Ultimately the resulting exposures will need to be fed into interest rate risk appetite.

Risk Monitoring

Aside from monitoring exposures against appetite, insurers may monitor KRIs such as benchmark yields (e.g. a 10-year swap rate) as a proxy for interest rate changes to data; and the average duration of assets and liabilities separately as a measure of how well these are matched. Note that average duration may mask mismatches at different points of the curve and there needs to supplementary monitoring of matches by term bands.

Risk Management

Insurers may be able to match liability proceeds exactly with cash flows, thus hedging out interest rate risk. Alternatively, they may use immunization techniques to guard against changes in the yield curve, choosing assets with the same duration as and wider convexity than liabilities. Although easier to implement, this approach requires assets to be regularly rebalanced. It is also vulnerable to nonparallel yield curve shifts. A compromise approach would be to split asset and liability cash flows into term bands and ensure that cash flows in each band are matched.

Interest rate swaps increase the flexibility available to insurers to match cash flows. Often they can be applied as an overlay to nonbond assets, hedging out interest rate risk in respect of liabilities while leaving a residual mismatch between asset proceeds and cash obligations under the swap.

Note that even if assets are in cash, there will be residual risk to differences between deposit rates and the LIBOR and other benchmark rates in which obligations are expressed. As well as swaps, interest rate swaptions can be used to hedge the cost of interest rate-related guarantees such as guaranteed annuity rates.

Summary and Further Steps

The article has set out some pointers as to how an insurer may optimally manage market risk, but there is no single ideal framework. Insurers will face a wide variety of risks depending on the countries and markets in which they operate. Whatever framework they put in place should be commensurate with the amount and complexity of the market risks they face.

However, the financial crisis taught many insurers bitter lessons about their market risk exposures, and there are no grounds for complacency. Market risk frameworks should be robust enough to identify and cope with new risks that emerge. Insurers should never consider their framework to be final but should always be looking to improve it.

It is recommended that insurers consider the following.

- Market risk classification should be reviewed for granularity and for any ambiguity between market risks and other risks. The UK actuarial profession's classification system (Kelliher *et al.*, 2011) could help in this assessment.

- Are market risk policy requirements embedded in investment management agreements? How strong is the governance over asset managers?

- How are new market risks relating to products identified? How would the insurer identify new asset types or material changes in existing classes?

- What process is in place to identify emerging market and other risks?

- How integrated are internal models with the wider risk management framework? How are these reviewed and updated for new products and asset types, or for changes in existing risks?

- How is market risk monitored? Does this consider breaches of market risk controls as well as quantitative KRIs?

- What are the limitations of the techniques used to manage market risk?

More Info

Market risk is a very broad topic and it would be impossible to list all relevant papers and texts. The author recommends the following sample of books and papers to those wishing to know more about market risk and its management.

Books:

Ferguson, Adam. *When Money Dies: The Nightmare of Deficit Spending, Devaluation, and Hyperinflation in Weimar Germany.* New York: Public Affairs, 2010.

Galbraith, John Kenneth. *The Great Crash 1929.* New York: Houghton Mifflin, 2009. A classic account of financial disaster.

Hull, John C. *Options, Futures, and Other Derivatives.* 8th ed. Upper Saddle River, NJ: Prentice Hall, 2011. Seminal textbook covering derivatives and the risks associated with these.

Reinhart, Carmen M., and Kenneth S. Rogoff. *This Time Is Different: Eight Centuries of Financial Folly.* Princeton, NJ: Princeton University Press, 2011. Excellent coverage of financial crises, putting these into their historical and geographical perspective.

Sweeting, Paul. *Financial Enterprise Risk Management.* Cambridge, UK: Cambridge University Press, 2011. Textbook on market risk and wider financial risk management, giving a sound grounding in quantitative techniques for modeling these.

Taleb, Nassim Nicholas. *Fooled by Randomness: The Hidden Role of Chance in Life and in the Markets.* New York: Random House, 2005. An interesting read with some profound insights into financial market behavior.

Reports:

Besar, D., P. Booth, K. K. Chan, A. K. L. Milne, and J. Pickles. "Systemic risk in financial services." Institute and Faulty of Actuaries, November 27, 2009. Online at: tinyurl.com/ms2brou. Paper on systemic risks and how market and other risks may be amplified.

Derivatives Working Party of the Institute and Faculty of Actuaries. "Credit derivatives." Institute and Faculty of Actuaries, January 26, 2006. Online at: tinyurl.com/lw66pe8

Eason, Scott, William Diffey, Ross Evans, Paul Fulcher, and Tim Wilkins. "Does your hedge do what it says on the tin? Hedging strategies for insurers: Effectiveness in recent conditions and regulatory treatment." Staple Inn Actuarial Society, April 13, 2010. Online at: www.sias.org.uk/view_paper?id=April2010talk

Frankland, Ralph, Andrew D. Smith, Timothy Wilkins, Elliot Varnell, Andy Holtham, Enrico Biffis, Seth Eshun, and David Dullaway. "Modelling extreme market events." Institute and Faculty of Actuaries, October 22, 2008. Online at: tinyurl.com/mvycwyd. Paper by the UK actuarial profession's benchmarking stochastic models working party, with particularly good coverage of equity market falls.

Kelliher, P. O. J., D. Wilmot, J. Vij, and P. J. M. Klumpes. "A common risk classification system for the actuarial profession." Institute and Faculty of Actuaries, October 31, 2011. Online at: tinyurl.com/mgrz82j; accompanying spreadsheet: tinyurl.com/jvtdxvl

Lazzari, Shaun, Celine Wong, and Peter Mason. "Dimension reduction techniques and forecasting interest rates." Staple Inn Actuarial Society, July 17, 2012. Online at: www.sias.org.uk/diary/view_meeting?id=SIASMeetingJuly12. Includes useful coverage of the PCA technique widely used in modeling yield curves.

Maher, J., J. Corrigan, A. Bentley, and W. Diffey. "An executive's handbook for understanding and risk managing unit linked guarantees." Institute and Faculty of Actuaries, October 20, 2010. Online: tinyurl.com/m6tfahd

---

1 Disclosure: I lead the working party which produced this paper and accompanying spreadsheet.

2 See SYSC 16.1 of the sourcebook: fsahandbook.info/FSA/html/handbook/SYSC/16/1

3 As an example of changes in the nature of an existing asset class, between 2000 and 2007, the home equity loan content of new US CDO issues increased from 5% to 36%. This increased concentration ultimately lead to elevated default experience and catastrophic loss in value. See Anna Katherine Barnett-Hart. "The story of the CDO market meltdown: An empirical analysis." March 19, 2009. Online at: tinyurl.com/m3mqhd9 [PDF].

4 On October 31, 2012, for example, HSBC accounted for 7.6% of the FTSE 100 Index and 6.5% of the FT All Share Index; see www.ftse.com/Indices/UK_Indices/index.jsp

5 Based on quarterly FT All Share Index price–equity ratios from 1988 to 2011; see tinyurl.com/mu6jmgt

Solvency II—
A New Regulatory Framework for the Insurance Sector

by Paul Barrett and Daniel Byrne

This Chapter Covers

- The aims of Solvency II.
- Setting risk-based capital requirements.
- Embedding risk management.
- Current timeline for implementation.
- Solvency II's impact on global insurance supervision.

Overview

Solvency II is a pan-European regulatory framework which, as described by the now replaced UK Financial Services Authority, "aims to establish a revised set of EU-wide capital requirements, valuation techniques, and risk management standards" to replace the current Solvency I regime. It will apply to all insurance companies across the EU with a gross premium income exceeding €5 million.

In being developed at the European level, Solvency II aims to implement a level playing field of insurance regulation (a concept referred to as "maximum harmonization") and as a whole improve the quality and focus of the supervision of the insurance industry across the region.

The Structure

One of the features of Solvency II that most have heard of but may not be entirely clear on is the "Three Pillars" approach. In short, Pillar 1 involves insurance companies demonstrating that they have adequate resources to support the business that they are writing. Pillar 2 revolves around systems of governance and in particular firms fully embedding a comprehensive Risk Management Framework, while Pillar 3 focuses on both regulatory reporting and public disclosure requirements.

The most important feature of Solvency II is that it is a risk-based regulatory regime: Capital requirements are related to the risk profile of an insurance entity, instead of being set in an arbitrary way on a country-by-country basis by the national regulators and legislators. Higher risks will lead to a higher capital requirement. Solvency II allows firms to calculate their risk based capital requirement (Solvency Capital Requirement of SCR) either through a set pan-industry calculation (Standard Formula) or through an "Internal Model," an entity specific capital calculation.

It should be noted that firms can only calculate their SCR with an Internal Model if they have received approval from their local regulator. Given the role capital modeling (under Basel II) had in the 2008 financial crises, the level of regulatory review (both initially and on an ongoing basis) of firms' internal models will be comprehensive and the burden is placed on the firm to demonstrate their Internal Model provides an appropriate reflection of their risk profile. The SCR is the first threshold of regulatory capital, the Minimum Capital Requirement (or MCR) is the ultimate back-stop and is consistently calculated for all firms. Where a firm breaches the MCR it can expect significant regulatory intervention, including the being closed to write new business.

A second feature of the Solvency II framework is a greater focus on insurance groups (as opposed to separate legal entities). The existing Solvency I regime, being on a state-by-state basis, finds it impossible to consider groups operating on a pan-European basis, from the perspective of group capital adequacy.

The third key feature is the increased focus on Risk Management and in particular the development of the "Own Risk and Solvency Assessment" (ORSA). The ORSA requires firms to bring together their business planning, capital plan and risk management framework to assess and understand their key drivers of risk both at the point in time and on a forward looking basis (3–5 year time horizon).

Timeline to Implementation

In July 2007, the European Union (EU) introduced the Framework Directive for Solvency II (the first of three "levels" of regulatory requirements). The new regulatory regime aims to be a "modern, risk-based, supervisory framework for the regulation of European insurance and reinsurance companies."

Since the publication of the Solvency II Directive there have however been multiple false starts in the implementation of Solvency II. Not only have Levels 2 and 3 (the more granular regulatory requirements) not been finalized, but in fact following the ratification of the Treaty of Lisbon, the Level 1 Solvency II Directive itself has had to be redrafted to align with legislative developments in the EU. What started as a straightforward update to the legalese of the directive has in fact opened a Pandora's Box of national interest and industry uncertainty. The challenges of setting a consistent regulatory framework that improves prudential regulation across the diverse insurance markets of Europe has proved a significant hurdle.

The latest timeline for Solvency II realistically sets implementation at January 2016 or potentially later. In the interim period the European Insurance and Occupational Pensions Authority (EIOPA) have produced a set of guidelines for national regulators to transition their industries to the Solvency II regime. For example the Prudential Regulation Authority (PRA), the successor to the FSA, are utilizing their Individual Capital Assessment (ICA) framework to continue to assess firms Internal Models, and readiness for Solvency II.

The EIOPA Guidelines for transitioning to Solvency II focus on a number of the more stable aspects of the regulations, namely, Internal Model Pre-Application, Systems of Governance, ORSA and Reporting requirements. The guidelines require national regulators to assess firm preparedness from 2014 onwards across each of these areas.

Impacts Further Afield— Setting New Global Standards

The key facets of Solvency are at the leading edge of global insurance supervision. Accordingly the global representative of insurance regulators, the International Association of Insurance Supervisors (IAIS), has utilized aspects on Solvency II within its Insurance Core Principles (ICP) initiative. National regulators that are members of the IAIS are required to comply with these high-level ICPs. As such one of the Solvency II Requirements that has reached the global stage is the ORSA. Countries including the United States, Canada, Bermuda, Singapore, Mexico, and others are currently developing and in some cases implementing their own ORSA requirements.

Conclusion

Whilst there is still uncertainty around the final implementation date of the full Solvency II regulatory regime, activity at the national supervisory level continues with local regulators implementing and embedding aspects of the framework in preparation for implementation. In spite of the costs of preparing for Solvency II to date, the benefits it has provided to the industry should not be underestimated. Expediting firms' modeling capabilities and hence understanding of their risk profile has yielded a powerful tool in the form of the internal model. The ability to more accurately assess and price risk results in real benefits throughout the operations of insurance firms. From being a key input in underwriting decisions to optimizing reinsurance structures and investment portfolios.

As such aspects of Solvency II such as the Internal Model and ORSA should be seen as more than just regulatory exercises and more as fundamental risk management tools to aid all aspects of the business. So in spite of the delays and uncertainty in the Solvency II regime itself, the principles that underlie it are already having real impacts in the insurance industry globally.

More Info

Websites:

Association of British Insurers on Solvency II: tinyurl.com/olez42t

European Union guidelines on Solvency II: tinyurl.com/2usz3wb

Enterprise Risk Management and Solvency II

by Andy Davies

This Chapter Covers

- The key components of enterprise risk management (ERM).
- The dangers of overcomplicating processes.
- How policies, risk strategy, and risk appetite are set.
- Capital allocation and management.
- The implications of Solvency II.

Introduction

There is a great deal that the insurance sector has to come to terms with as it addresses the implications of Solvency II. There are broad general questions such as: What does it all mean? How will it be achieved and its requirements met? How much will it cost, both from a capital and a monetary perspective? What resources are required? Then there is the related issue of how the International Financial Reporting Standards (IFRS) will fit with Solvency II.

Enterprise Risk Management: Culture Is the Key

Rating agencies, analysts, shareholders, and regulators are all taking more interest in capital models and enterprise risk management (ERM). Effective ERM acts as "the common thread that links balance sheet strength, operating performance, and business profile."[1]

In an ideal ERM model, the risk management group will work with the board and all employees to ensure that their organization has effective ERM. It is fair to say that the majority of companies today have some form of ERM, but it is also true that for many this is an area that needs further development.

ERM is not about finding the perfect model; it is about having a strong risk-management culture which ensures that risk is understood, controlled, and effectively communicated. Effective ERM should be part of an insurance company's DNA.

The key components of ERM are:

• aligning risk appetite and strategy;

• enhancing risk response decisions;

• reducing operational surprises and losses;

• identifying and managing multiple and cross-enterprise risks;

• seizing opportunities;

• improving the deployment of capital.

Management should consider the company's risk appetite in evaluating its strategy, setting objectives, and developing mechanisms to manage related risks. ERM provides the rigour to identify and select alternative responses to risk—such as risk avoidance, risk reduction, risk sharing, and risk acceptance. Through ERM, companies enhance their ability to identify potential events and establish responses, thereby reducing surprises and associated costs or losses.

Every company faces a variety of risks that affect different parts of the organization, and ERM facilitates effective responses to such multiple risks. By considering a full range of potential events, management can identify and proactively realize opportunities.

Finally, obtaining robust risk information allows management to assess overall capital needs effectively and enhance capital allocation.

ERM and Solvency II

Solvency II is based on three "pillars." Pillar 1 is about capital requirements and the triggers for supervisory action. Pillar 2 focuses on the supervisory activities of regulators, based on organizational and governance requirements. Pillar 3 covers additional disclosures that supervisors may need to carry out their regulatory function. Under Solvency II, the concept of an "internal model" effectively refers to an enterprise-wide risk management framework. It covers both the quantitative requirements of Pillar 1 and the organizational and governance requirements of Pillar 2.

The broad thrust of an internal model is to use an economic capital model, accompanied by the embedding and effective management of risk, driven from the board to the front line.

It is important to remember the context and immediate historical backdrop against which the insurance sector is working. It is undeniable, for example, that the industry has had problems with risk assessment and modeling in recent years. The 2005 hurricane damage payouts and the credit crisis put significant stress on capital and liquidity requirements for many companies. This makes discussion of capital adequacy regimes a very strong necessity, not just an academic exercise.

However, as insurance company boards try to square up to these issues—and there are many of them—there is a real danger of overcomplicating certain processes and of critical data being obscured by information overload. Having a complex model is no guarantee of success, as the crises experienced by several banks will testify. Instead, what is really critical is to ensure that the insurer's approach to risk management is simple enough for all staff to understand and engage with, and that it is also effective enough to add real value. The concept of "proportionality" is specifically enshrined within the proposed European Directive for Solvency II, so there is regulatory recognition that we do not need to over-elaborate.

Risk management will only be fully effective if people throughout the organization receive clear, consistent messages from leadership and understand what they need to do. It starts at the top, and senior management need to develop a unified view, common language, policies, and appropriate governance structures.

The testimony of Paul Moore, former head of Group Regulatory Risk at HBOS, makes clear the importance of culture in risk management. Moore commented that: "Being an internal risk and compliance manager at the time felt a bit like being a man in a rowing boat trying to slow down an oil tanker."[2] If the culture is wrong, then even the most sophisticated model will be ineffective.

Markel Corporation, the company for which I work, is a relatively small company with 400 employees.[3] It therefore has a very flat organization structure, enabling close interaction between board and employees. This is very helpful as all employees can be given clear and consistent messages in a common language. We are committed to creating an environment in which risk is managed effectively. The Markel style, which articulates our core values, includes statements that "we will build the financial value of our company," which implies a steady, cautious approach to risk, and "we are encouraged to challenge management...we have the ability to make decisions or alter a course quickly," which empowers discussions of strategy. As both US and UK management "walk the talk," this culture facilitates a risk-focused approach for all employees.

Figure 1 highlights that a clear articulation of risk strategy and risk appetite is an essential starting point in embedding risk management across an organization. These statements of corporate objectives act as the fundamental reference point against which all risk-taking and risk-mitigation activity within an organization should be benchmarked. They provide governance and define boundaries within which risk-based decision-making can occur, and provide a clear framework for the selection of one course of action over another.

Figure 1. Insurer of the future with integrated model

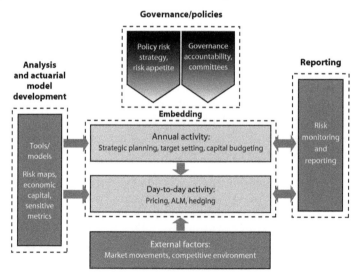

Policies, risk strategy, and risk appetite are set at board level, and this is embedded into the annual and day-to-day activities of the business. These activities are analyzed through various risk maps, capital models, and sensitivity metrics. In addition, external factors such as market movements and the actions of competitors are communicated to the business. The model at Markel that is shown in Figure 2 splits the business into two components—underwriting and investing. As a consequence there are several key committees and meetings. These are:

- IBNR (incurred but not reported losses) and P&L meetings, at which all aspects of underwriting and reserving are discussed;

- Investment Committee meetings, where all aspects of the company's investment performance and strategy are discussed;

- in the middle, the Capital and Risk Committees, which look at the company's risk and capital management.

Figure 2. Model used at Markel

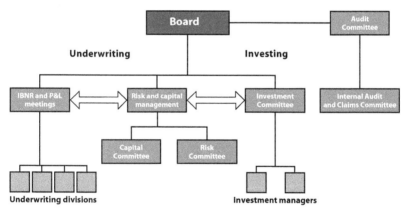

The IBNR and P&L meetings are crucial to the way Markel operates. A thorough and robust reserving process is the cornerstone of a successful organization. It is important that underwriters and management agree on the IBNR results as this ensures that there is one version of the truth. Having two sets of numbers causes confusion, wastes time, and results in poor decision-making.

The meetings need to be held on a consistent and regular basis. At Markel, IBNR meetings are held quarterly, and the P&L meetings are held on a monthly basis. The IBNR packs and P&L statements show the combined ratio and the required return on risk-adjusted capital by line of business. They include all allocated expenses so that the underwriters understand the full cost of writing their business.

The IBNR and P&L meetings are attended by senior management and underwriters and are a crucial part of the business culture at Markel. They are used to identify lines of business that are not achieving profitability and required return on capital targets so that appropriate action can be taken at the earliest opportunity.

It is crucial that the results of all these meetings are embedded in the management and financial reporting and also in the capital management of the business.

Finally, the activities and results of the business are fed back to the board through effective risk management and reporting.

The results are a key driver in deciding the remuneration of underwriters. Part of our underwriters' remuneration is phased over a period of years, which thus provides a safeguard against underwriting strategies that appear profitable in the short term but ultimately deteriorate. The alignment of risk management with remuneration strategy is an essential part of the effective embedding of ERM.

Capital Allocation and Management

The standard model for the majority of companies in the United Kingdom today is a product of the Individual Capital Assessment (ICA) regime, introduced by the Financial Services Authority while it waited for Europe to refine and introduce Solvency II. The implementation of ICA has been a significant step forward in delivering more risk-based capital management and has gone a good way to help meet the challenges of Solvency II.

Figure 3 highlights that for a nonlife company the basic capital requirement is split into four risk categories:

- insurance risk;
- liquidity risk;

- market risk;
- credit risk.

Figure 3. Capital allocation

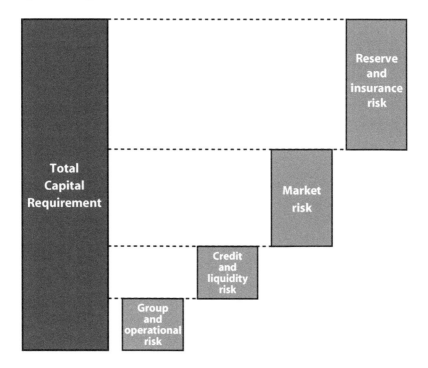

The capital assigned to these risk categories is used to produce the basic capital requirement of the company, and in most cases the capital required is calculated through a combination of stress and scenario tests and a capital model. Operational and group risk are added to the basic capital requirement to produce the company's total capital requirement.

Although this model has been successful in getting companies through the ICA regime, it will not be sufficient to meet the requirements of Solvency II. In addition, ICA models suffer from the fact that for the most part they have been developed and owned by the finance and actuarial departments in companies. As a consequence, there has been minimal embedding into the rest of the business. At Markel, our ICA process has always been multi-disciplined, with a number of stakeholders involved. However, we are embedding the process further. Individual members of the Capital and Risk Committee work with the board, underwriters, and investment managers to ensure that they understand the capital being allocated to them and the risk-adjusted returns required.

The key to effective capital management is to ensure:

- That it drives the decision-making process, ensuring optimal use of capital.

- That it is embedded into the business. It needs to be a key driver in strategy and planning, acquisitions, new lines of business, and legacy claims management. This is an area that needs a considerable amount of effort, but the benefits are considerable. This area is key to achieving the objectives of Solvency II.

- That people are rewarded by return on capital. People will take more of an interest if their bonuses are dependent on it, so ensure that the bonuses of underwriters and senior management are calculated by return on capital.

- That the model is transparent and well documented. Too many models act as a black box whose results cannot be explained.

- That financial and nonfinancial information used by the model and the capital management team is consistent with the information used by the business. Different information causes confusion, wastes time, and will result in poor decisions being made. An organization cannot have a model that operates with standalone information—it needs to be embedded into all aspects of the business.

The goal should be to minimize group and operational risk through effective ERM. A prudent approach is to have minimal appetite for credit and liquidity risk and a reasonable appetite for market risk.

The last and most significant risk is reserve and underwriting risk. A sound approach here is to split the capital required for reserve and underwriting risk into two components: prior-year reserve risk and current business risk. Here one allocates capital to cover the uncertainty on prior-year insurance reserves. Again, one can try to reduce this capital requirement by establishing prudent case and IBNR reserves so that reserves are more likely to be redundant than deficient.

Capital is also allocated to underwriting the current business. This capital is allocated to each product line, enabling management to set combined ratio targets that achieve the required return on risk-adjusted capital. These combined ratio targets will vary according to the volatility, length of tail, and reinsurance usage of the product line. In addition, the combined ratio target will take into consideration diversification with other classes of business.

The combined ratio targets are used to benchmark underwriting performance, and they act as a key driver in the setting of underwriter and management bonus targets.

What Are the Implications of Solvency II?

The three-pillar approach of Solvency II works as follows. Pillar 1 deals with the quantitative capital requirements. It ensures that the valuation of assets and liabilities, and the calculation of capital requirements, are standardized. The areas covered are:

- valuation of technical provisions;
- minimum capital requirement;
- solvency capital requirement;
- investment rules.

Pillar 2 deals with the qualitative side of Solvency II and focuses on

- the principles of internal control and risk management;
- individual risk and capital assessment;
- the supervisory review process.

Pillar 3 deals with disclosure requirements discipline and covers:

- transparency and disclosure and the support of risk-based supervision through market mechanisms.

So what are the implications of Solvency II for capital management? Already we can see that there are problems.

Within Pillar 1 it is clear that the technical provision under Solvency II and IFRS is calculated differently. This difference will be a potent source of confusion, additional cost, and wasted effort—and it needs to be resolved.

It is also clear that the communications effort required to implement Pillar 1 will not be trivial. How are the new technical provisions to be communicated and embedded in the business? How do you explain to underwriters that their loss ratio reflects discounting and a cost-of-capital adjustment? It took a long time for underwriters to understand combined ratios, so this will be a challenge.

The minimum capital requirement (MRC) set out in Solvency II fails to reward appropriate risk management due to its formulaic approach. It is also clear that in the majority of cases an internal capital model produces a lower solvency capital requirement, which means that there is a significant advantage to an organization in having its model approved. Finally, there are also significant implications for IT and data collection.

With Pillar 2 it is crucial that a company can demonstrate that it has effective ERM and that it is embedded in the business. Meeting the embedding or "use test" requires significant time and resources.

The main focus of Pillar 3 is disclosure, and therefore the implications of these disclosures need to be carefully thought through. These disclosures will include a report on:

- governance and risk management;

- valuation principles applied for solvency purposes;

- the internal model: methodologies, assumptions, and validation;

- capital requirements, with an account of the company's minimum capital requirement and solvency capital requirement (SCR) and any breaches during the year, plus a breakdown of the SCR standard formula and internal model calculations.

Conclusion

So how does the road ahead look? It is clear that the sector has a number of challenges to overcome and that a period of hard work lies ahead. An effective ERM model, as we have argued throughout this piece, should be fundamental to any approach to implementing Solvency II and will, of itself, bring tremendous benefits to organizations that work to embed ERM in their organization.

Summary and Further Steps

- A strong management culture will ensure that risks are understood, controlled, and effectively communicated. Effective ERM is a key driver in Solvency II.

- It is crucial that capital and risk management are embedded in the business. These are the DNA of an insurance company.

- Return on risk-adjusted capital should be a key driver in the remuneration of underwriters and management.

- Considerable resources and expense are still required to develop a fully integrated model; however, the capital benefits of doing so will be significant.

More Info

Websites:

European Commission on Solvency II:
ec.europa.eu/internal_market/insurance/solvency/index_en.htm

Financial Services Authority (FSA; UK) on Solvency II:
www.fsa.gov.uk/pages/About/What/International/solvency/index.shtml

Solvency II Association training and presentations: www.solvency-ii-training.com

---

1 AM Best. "Risk management and the rating process for insurance companies." January 25, 2008. Online at: www.ambest.com/ratings/methodology/riskmanagement.pdf

2 Paul Moore, HBOS. "Man in a rowing boat."

3 Markel International comprises the international operations of Markel Corporation, a US property casualty company listed on the New York Stock Exchange. It writes a variety of property, casualty, and marine insurance and reinsurance business through its two London-based platforms: Markel International Insurance Company and Markel Syndicate 3000.

Own Risk and Solvency Assessment (ORSA): Strategy, People, and Complexity

by Neil Cantle

This Chapter Covers
- The integral nature of strategy and risk.
- Risk management as a tool to identify and understand the uncertainty inherent in your strategy.
- People who are at the heart of risk management.
- How to harness expert input within risk management.
- How to assess and understand "complex" risks.

Introduction

Modern risk management is hard. The difficulty arises primarily because modern business is complex. When we look at the strategy our business is trying to deliver we see a forest of multiple factors—which depend on other factors, which in turn interact with others. It really is hard to "see the wood for the trees" and make sense of it all. This chapter explains how to make sense of modern risk and the role that people play within it, and it provides an overview of the tools available to modern risk managers to cut through this complexity.

Strategy and Risk

Around the world, many insurers are being asked to plan for the completion of "own risk and solvency assessment" (ORSA) style exercises. Although the details vary slightly in each country, the primary purpose is rather similar—to identify the risks inherent in your organization and to ensure that you have the resources and know how to manage them appropriately.

Strategy is all about the identification of a direction for the company, with associated goals, and an idea of how you are going to get there. The chosen strategy usually reflects some aspect of differentiation from the competition, such as: the use of skills or resources which you feel you can deploy better than your competitors; or a product that in some way is more attractive than competitors' products.

The achievement of strategic goals is rarely a certain outcome. The reality of the business world means that, although they should be somewhat clustered around the planned outcome, the actual results could be quite different to what was planned. Some of these outcomes could be welcome outperformance, but many will not—and risk represents the possibility of these unwelcome outcomes.

The development of the risk management discipline has been an ongoing journey of finding ways to identify the sources of uncertainty associated with the pursuit of corporate goals and seeking ways to "optimize" the chances of being successful through risk mitigation, management, or avoidance. Historically, the focus has been very much on avoiding or controlling risk, but in recent years this has evolved to incorporate an understanding of which risks are being sought in return for rewards or accepted in the pursuit of these. Through the use of mechanisms such as risk appetite, companies are seeking to ensure that they take the risks they intend to and earn appropriate rewards for taking them. This moves risk management forward from being a pure "control" or "compliance" exercise toward being an integral part of the strategic planning and performance management processes of the business.

Making Sense of Complexity

So how should one go about trying to unearth the uncertainties that are inherent in a modern insurance company and make sense of them?

A good place to start is to understand what you are trying to achieve: the amount of profit; the stability of profit; the capital coverage required; market positioning; or environmental behavior. For each of these goals there will be a—possibly wide—range of potential outcomes depending on how things work out in practice as you try to implement your strategy. The second step is therefore to understand what ranges of outcomes are possible for each of these goals. Describing your risk appetite[1] requires you to determine how much risk you *can* take ("risk capacity") and then to determine how much risk you are *prepared to* take ("risk tolerance") for each source of risk ("risk preferences"). The articulation of risk appetite is therefore at the heart of exercises like ORSA as it explains the types, and amounts, of uncertainties that you wish to be exposed to in pursuing your chosen strategy. To operationalize the concept, however, it is necessary to understand what generates those uncertainties and assign operational parameters to help the organization to know the boundaries of day-to-day activities.

For this, an understanding of the ranges of outcomes is insufficient— we also need to know how undesirable outcomes could occur if we are to stand any chance of influencing them. But this is where things get hard: surely there could be an infinite number of ways in which the profit we end up with might not be the figure we had planned? Well, yes, quite probably.

Complex phenomena have been studied by a number of disciplines outside of the business world, and it turns out that the insights from these are helpful for us here. To utilize them we need to introduce the concept of "systems." In this context, a "system" is defined as "a set of two or more components that are interconnected for a purpose." Mitleton-Kelly (2003) describes complexity as the interrelationship, interaction, and interconnectivity of elements within a system and between the system and its environment. Modern companies are nearly always complex adaptive systems. As described in Allan *et al.* (2013), "For complex systems, like an economy or financial organizations, a new paradigm or philosophy is required to understand how the constituent parts interact to create behaviors not predictable from the 'sum of the parts.' Systems theory provides a more robust conceptual framework which views risk as an emerging property arising from the complex and adaptive interactions which occur within companies, sectors and economies."

Blockley (2005) describes the role of "systems thinking" as being "to integrate the language of uncertainty and complexity and its expression in risk, as well as managing risk in terms of two systems—the 'hard' embedded in the 'soft.'" Here, "hard" systems are described by Checkland (1993) as being "characterized by the ability to define purpose, goals and missions that can be addressed via engineering methodologies in attempting to, in some sense, 'optimize' a solution." The concept of "soft" systems was added later, being those "characterized by extremely complex, problematical and often mysterious phenomena for which concrete goals cannot be established and which require learning in order to make improvement."

It is easy to see that companies involve large components of these "soft" systems—and yet many of the risk management tools that are being used are typically designed for "hard" systems.

Figure 1. Seeing beneath the surface

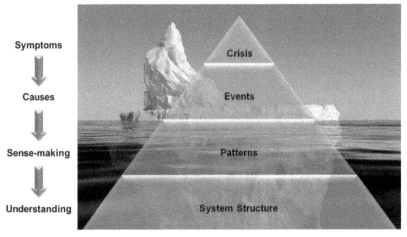

People traditionally focus a lot of energy on the visible part of risk and uncertainty—the part above the water in Figure 1. They identify undesirable outcomes ("crises") and seek to identify their "causes"—i.e. the events which lead to them. The information collected at this level is often categorized and stored in databases in the belief that it can help to inform predictions of future trends. This is a classic "hard" systems approach.

But why are these databases often such poor predictors of the future? This is because we are still a way from understanding "why" particular events have taken place—we simply know that they did and what some of the potential consequences might be. We need to look deeper, and consider the part of the iceberg below the water in Figure 1. We have to seek out the patterns that will help us to make sense of how the events might be related in some way, and ultimately seek an understanding of the underlying mechanism which produces them. People are generally afraid to venture "beneath the water" as they believe that the complex outcomes we see are surely the result of impenetrably complex dynamics and that describing them at this level would be impossible or too prohibitively complex to be useful.

Complex adaptive systems have some basic properties (see Sidebar 1) which help to highlight some important misconceptions and myths about the behaviors of complex systems. These mean that some of the techniques that are typically used can actually be misleading in dangerous ways.

> Basic properties of complex adaptive systems:
>
> • systems have a purpose;
>
> • emergence: the whole has properties that do not originate in the subcomponents;
>
> • self-organization: they have structure and hierarchy but few leverage points;
>
> • interacting feedback loops cause highly nonlinear behavior;
>
> • they are characterized by counterintuitive and unintended consequences;
>
> • they have a tipping point or critical complexity limit before collapse;
>
> • they evolve, and history is important;
>
> • cause and symptom are separated in time and space.

The first error is thinking that a complex systems problem is best solved by reducing it to a series of simpler parts. The outcomes of complex systems are emergent, arising from the interactions of many underlying parts, and the understanding of these interactions is crucial to understanding the system overall. So, unlike merely complicated systems, complex systems cannot be reduced and must be studied holistically first. The second major error is in classifying historical behaviors using basic identifiers and applying statistical analyses to these groups—such groupings are often neither homogeneous nor driven by the same mechanism over time, making the use of statistical analysis problematic. We therefore need a way to understand what is actually going on before we try to simplify our information or models.

People at the Heart of Risk Management

There is an inescapable link between people and risk. "Much of the real mess that keeps the beautiful equations and ERM systems from working perfectly comes from people," says David Ingram (2010). Companies are essentially social constructs comprising people all of whom are trying to follow processes and procedures to achieve the particular goals of their organization. As they go about their work, their performance is going to be subject to variation—deliberate or otherwise—that introduces myriad complexities into the system.

But people are not just passive parts of the system. They are often actively trying to anticipate the behavior of systems and to influence them. Even in today's technological environment, few companies truly have immediate information about the consequences of their actions; it takes time for actions to unfold, causing feedback loops and complex subsystems. It also turns out that humans are generally not good at solving the types of problems that are usually posed in risk assessment, and so their interventions nearly always have unintended consequences.

In trying to simplify the risk problems that we face, we tend to make assumptions about the behavior of others. In particular, it is often assumed that everyone is behaving rationally and that their behaviors are consistent over time. Neither of these things will actually tend to be true! In fact studies show that:

- humans cannot be rational, even when they try to be;

- even when they can be rational, they aren't;

- humans prefer to use other tools for decision-making, such as emotion, gut feel, or suspicion.

People suffer from a number of further cognitive shortcomings when we look at their role in risk assessment. Tversky and Kahneman (1974) describe the "cognitive biases that stem from the reliance on judgmental heuristics" and the fact that "statistical principles are not learned from everyday experience." People are fundamentally poor at assessing probability (Fenton and Neil (2013) present a good series of examples of how people get this wrong), and yet we consistently rely on expert opinions in our risk management activity—even models that have been "factually" calibrated against historical data rely on an expert's opinion that such a trend will continue into the future.

> "How do humans reason in situations that are complicated or ill-defined? Modern psychology tells us that as humans we are only moderately good at deductive logic, and we make only moderate use of it. But we are superb at seeing or recognizing or matching patterns—behaviors that confer obvious evolutionary benefits. In problems of complication, then, we look for patterns." (Arthur, 1994)

The mental models people use to make sense of the world have a bias toward optimism, making it hard for them to see the need for change, and so there is a tendency to inertia and trying to keep doing the same thing—a behavior we saw a lot of during the onset of the recent global financial crisis. There is also a natural bias toward loss aversion, giving an asymmetric assessment of risk. Recent risk-taking experience will also have a significant impact on the way individuals balance perceived risk and reward, so that the same situation viewed at different times could lead to quite different courses being taken.

Another big challenge is that in a stable environment mental models become increasingly effective at the expense of flexibility. Stable environments therefore naturally select resources with skills optimized for that environment, further reducing future flexibility. This process of specialization and optimization forms part of an adaptive cycle of system life, described by Gunderson and Holling (2002). As a company becomes increasingly optimized and forgoes resources which assist flexibility, it becomes increasingly fragile and exposed to changes in the environment. A number of companies found this to their cost during the recent global financial crisis as they were unable to respond to severe changes in liquidity and investment conditions as well as shock changes in customer behaviors. In areas such as ecology it has increasingly become known that resilience[2] is a far more sensible target to aim for than optimization when you are dealing with complex systems, but it does require short-term inefficiency by investing in resources which preserve flexibility.

Culture, or rather organizational behavior, plays a crucial role in risk management too. The prevailing behavioral environment can have profound impacts on the way in which risks arise and how they are identified, assessed, and managed. In particular, there is no single "mood" or culture at any point in time, but rather a dynamic and evolving blend of four risk attitudes, as embodied in the four character types described by Ingram and Thompson (2011):

- *pragmatists*, who believe that the world is uncertain and unpredictable;

- *conservators*, whose world is one of peril and high risk;

- *maximizers*, who see the world as low-risk and fundamentally self-correcting;

- *managers*, whose world is risky, but not too risky for firms that are guided properly.

In the context of enterprise risk management we therefore need to understand which blend of risk attitudes we have at any point in time and the drivers that lead them to change from one to another.

When studying the risk culture of organizations it is important not to base analyses solely on individuals' attitudes to risk. The overall culture, or that of subgroups, is an emergent property of the group and is therefore different to how someone might behave on their own. It also does not make sense to judge the culture against some allegedly "perfect" risk culture, since it is almost impossible to describe the many combinations of interacting subgroup cultures that would result in "perfect" risk management. It is, however, very helpful to understand the culture associated with the particular groups and processes within your organization so that you can design your risk framework to fit well with it and thus dramatically improve the embeddedness of your risk management.

So, people are at the heart of generating complexity and the failure to understand its meaning for risk. All is not lost, however—there is a range of techniques that can be used to make sense of these things.

Harnessing Expert Input

"Make things as simple as possible, but no simpler."

Albert Einstein

We have seen that people are not necessarily the best source of information about risk—but they are often the only source of information. This is particularly the case when events are rare or where emerging trends can be imagined to a new conclusion that has not been seen before—historical data will have little or nothing to add to the analysis of such situations, and yet these are precisely the ones that most risk managers are faced with on a daily basis. It is possible to recover the collective insights of your experts using cognitive techniques, like cognitive mapping (Eden, 1988) (see Sidebar 3 for a brief overview of cognitive mapping), and use these to distill a robust and meaningful insight of what is happening. The accompanying case study explains how this can work.

Cognitive Mapping

In your head you form a view of the world that is helpful to you in making sense of the complexities around you. It is possible to recover these images by reformulating narratives about particular topics as cognitive maps. Each node on the map represents a "concept" in the narrative, and the links between nodes represent the connections that you make between these concepts. So, for example, the sentence "increasing life spans is causing a strain on retirement income" could be represented by the linked nodes "increasing life spans" and "strain on retirement income."

Such maps can contain hundreds of nodes, but the structure of the map lends itself to rigorous analysis which can identify the most connected parts of the narrative (immediately or more globally) and the nodes that most often lead to such important concepts. It can also enable the identification of biases from the respondents and missing elements of the narrative. Narratives from multiple sources can be combined into a single coherent view of the problem.

The use of cognitive maps to capture and analyze the narrative of your experts provides a rigorous and robust way to form a coherent single story. Analyzing this map enables you to: determine areas of bias; identify missing story elements; and create a minimally complex summary of their narrative. From this you can form a deep understanding of the most important dynamics of your risk profile to feed into a wide range of risk management activity.

Case Study

Cognitive Mapping in Practice

Organization XYZ operates a strategy which exposes it to a wide range of stakeholders and it operates its business using a mixture of internal and outsourced processes. Balancing the needs of such a wide range of stakeholders is complicated and fraught with biases and different agendas.

The stakeholders were interviewed in small groups, each being asked to describe how the business went about delivering its strategic goals and what types of challenges were encountered. Each narrative looked at the story from a slightly different angle and used language that was meaningful to the storyteller, but not necessarily consistent with the phrases used by others. Converting these narratives into cognitive maps enabled the risk team to identify areas where the various stakeholders were using different language to describe the same concepts, and to identify parts of the narrative where some stakeholders had views that conflicted with those of others. Resolving these perspectives into a single cognitive map permitted a single view of the dynamics that drove strategic outcomes.

The cognitive map was analyzed to generate a minimally complex summary of the core features which explained the top dozen key features of the strategy, the interrelationships between them, and the storylines that most often led to these critical factors. Creating scenarios centered on these areas allowed the board and senior management to determine the more detailed factors that could cause these trigger points to be hit and to assess areas where existing controls were well aligned and where additional vigilance might be warranted. In particular, the analysis and discussion uncovered a number of scenarios where a series of relatively benign conditions might combine to create a potentially fatal situation for the organization.

Assessing and Understanding Complex Risks

We know from our discussion about systems thinking that reaching an understanding of the mechanism of a system is crucial if we are to make any kind of progress in assessing the risks that can emerge from it. In the real world we are nearly always faced with large gaps in our data relating to any but the most frequent observations, so a cognitive method for arriving at our first understanding of the system is invaluable.

There are now a number of additional factors that we can consider in trying to assess and understand our risks. First, we can attempt to build models which replicate the interesting dynamics that our experts have explained. The benefits of using a cognitive approach before proceeding to modeling are described, for example, by Cantle *et al.* (2013): "...financial stresses are serious, but the political and reputational aspects of [the organization's] critical success factors mean that failure could very well come from other directions...Actuarial models are very powerful...however, for reverse stress testing the challenge is to know which scenarios should be considered...The model simply cannot tell us which scenarios to look at. We must decide which scenarios to look at ourselves and then use the model to evaluate them."

If we have sufficient data, statistical models may well be capable of mimicking outcomes, but they have nothing to say about the drivers of such outcomes. As described by Fenton and Neil (2013), it is far more productive to consider causal models, such as Bayesian networks, which "help us to make sense of how risks emerge, are connected, and how we might represent our control and mitigation of them." In particular, we would like to be consistent in the way that we handle uncertainty when we study our risks, meaning that we have to find a way to incorporate subjective judgments about uncertainty. We also need to be able to revise our views when new evidence is observed. The Bayesian approach permits a subjective view of uncertainty which enables us to make much better progress with our risk studies than the classic frequentist approach that typical statistics requires.

Summary and Further Steps

- Modern businesses are complex and are properly described as "complex adaptive systems."

- They are also inextricably linked to humans, so it is virtually impossible to tackle any "enterprise"-level study without taking into account the human factor.

- The perfect rationality and information of *homo economicus* does not exist, and most of us suffer from a range of biases and shortcomings in the way we think about and assess risk.

- The tools of systems thinking and the complexity sciences offer a robust and rigorous way for us to make sense of the complex interactions that take place within our companies.

- The use of cognitive methods as a way to harness the input from experts enables significant progress even when data are scarce or trends are new.

- Structural models retain a useful connection between outcomes and drivers that can greatly assist the communication and understanding of risk dynamics in a business, while also more easily compensating for, or correcting, the cognitive biases that are inevitably present when engaging humans in risk management evaluations.

- Insights from anthropology (e.g. Thompson, 2008) and other related areas provide ways to understand how we should better align the design of our risk frameworks with the cultural features of our business. You need to be aware that there will be several cultures within your business at any one time, and that combinations of different types of risk management approach may be needed to truly embed enterprise risk management within the organization.

More Info

Books:

Blockley, D. I. *New Dictionary of Civil Engineering*. London, UK: Penguin, 2005.

Checkland, Peter. *Systems Thinking, Systems Practice*. Chichester, UK: Wiley, 1993.

Fenton, Norman, and Martin Neil. *Risk Assessment and Decision Analysis with Bayesian Networks*. Boca Raton, FL: CRC Press, 2013.

Gunderson, Lance H., and C. S. Holling (eds). *Panarchy: Understanding Transformations in Human and Natural Systems*. Washington, DC: Island Press, 2002.

Mitleton-Kelly, Eve. "Ten principles of complexity & enabling infrastructures." In Mitleton-Kelly, Eve (ed). *Complex Systems and Evolutionary Perspectives of Organisations: The Application of Complexity Theory to Organisations*. Oxford, UK: Elsevier, 2003. Online at: tinyurl.com/lcq6vlr [PDF].

Thompson, Michael. *Organising & Disorganising: A Dynamic and Non-Linear Theory of Institutional Emergence and its Implications*. Axminster, UK: Triarchy Press, 2008.

Articles:

Allan, Neil, Neil Cantle, Patrick Godfrey, and Yun Yin. "A review of the use of complex systems applied to risk appetite and emerging risks in ERM practice." *British Actuarial Journal* 18:1 (March 2013): 163–234. Online at: tinyurl.com/k6hhwqq [PDF].

Arthur, W. Brian. "Inductive reasoning and bounded rationality (the El Farol problem)." *American Economic Review* 84:2 (May 1994): 406–411. Online at: tuvalu.santafe.edu/~wbarthur/Papers/El_Farol.pdf

Cantle, Neil, Jean-Pierre Charmaille, Martin Clarke, and Lucy Currie. "An application of modern social sciences techniques to reverse stress testing at the UK Pension Protection Fund." Enterprise Risk Management Symposium, Chicago, April 22–24, 2013. Online at: www.ermsymposium.org/2013/pdf/erm-2013-paper-clarke.pdf

Eden, Colin. "Cognitive mapping: A review." *European Journal of Operational Research* 36:1 (July 1988): 1–13. Online at: dx.doi.org/10.1016/0377-2217(88)90002-1

Ingram, David. "The human dynamics of the credit crisis and implications for the afterlife." *Wilmott* (January 2010).

Ingram, David, and Michael Thompson. "Changing seasons of risk attitudes." *Actuary* 8:1 (February/March 2011): 20–24. Online at: tinyurl.com/lb324qd [PDF].

Tversky, Amos, and Daniel Kahneman. "Judgment under uncertainty: Heuristics and biases." *Science* 185:4157 (September 27, 1974): 1124–1131. Online at: tinyurl.com/5n77sl [PDF].

---

1   Defined in Allan *et al.* (2013) as "our comfort and preference for accepting a series of interconnected uncertainties related to achieving our strategic goals."

2   The ability to adapt and change as the environment around you changes—in some sense a capacity to survive "unknown unknowns." Not to be confused with "robustness," which is the ability to continue functioning after part of the system is damaged.

ERM for Emerging Risks in General Insurance

by George C. Orros

This Chapter Covers

- An enterprise risk management (ERM) framework model.
- ERM is now accepted as being a part of any general insurer's *modus operandi*.
- Three case studies are presented: American International Group (AIG), Long Term Capital Management (LTCM), and the Bhopal pesticide plant, India, owned by a subsidiary of Union Carbide.
- With hindsight, many of the mistakes made by the case study companies were predictable. In practice the situation is not clear cut and responses are inevitably based on imperfect information.
- Conclusions from the case studies.

Introduction

This article focuses on the practical application of enterprise risk management (ERM) principles for general insurance undertakings in our world of "unknown unknowns" and the emergence of unexpected risks over time. Consideration is given to how the chief risk officer (CRO) can focus within an ERM risk and opportunity management framework, balancing risks against opportunities, while being resilient in the face of "unknown unknowns" and their emergence over time to become what are commonly referred to as the "known unknowns" and the "known knowns."

ERM has been around for many years and yet it has had a chequered history, only recently starting to be fully adopted by companies in the UK insurance and financial service markets and elsewhere around the world. Elements of ERM have also been applied throughout the UK public sector agencies, including the National Health Service and other government departments.

Continued development of the regulatory environment and the sophistication of risk analysis techniques have changed the approaches adopted by general insurance undertakings in the United Kingdom and internationally. ERM is now commonly accepted as being a necessary part of any successful general insurer's *modus operandi*, even if what "good ERM" means is not generally understood. ERM appears to be here to stay.

The empirical research used in this article is anchored in three well-documented case studies. These are the general insurance-related features of AIG (American International Group), LTCM (Long Term Capital Management), and Union Carbide. The results underlie the best-practice indications recommended for ERM practitioners.

Consideration has been given to the lessons learned and the early warning indicators that could (and perhaps should) have been used to detect the emerging risks in a timely manner and which could have influenced the CRO to have taken appropriate remedial action. It is recognized that, with the benefit of hindsight, many of the mistakes made by the case study companies appear predictable. In practice, however, in the heat of emerging reality, the situation is not so clear cut and responses are inevitably based on imperfect data and information.

Readers may find it useful to ask themselves the following questions while considering the material presented in this chapter.

- Which key risk indicators and early warning indicators would you have used, why would you have used them, and how would they have informed your decisions?

- How quickly would you have spotted the emergence of the unexpected event, and what would you have done about it?

- What evidence would you have needed to convince the CEO to take the appropriate remedial action before it was too late?

ERM Framework Model

This article assesses the case study experience with reference to an ERM framework model and associated concepts of risk and opportunity management. The reader can make reference to this section to help them to analyze the case study experience and to build their own response to each of the three questions.

Literature reviews of ERM characterize the process as essentially one of risk and opportunity management, as a cycle which involves the main board functions, namely policy formulation, strategic thinking, supervisory management and accountability, and their control cycles. This is shown in Figure 1.

Figure 1. Risk and opportunity management control cycle

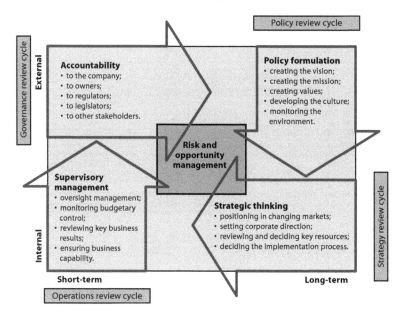

The control cycle can be further developed to form an ERM corporate governance model with the following elements:

- *corporate governance*–board oversight;
- *internal control*–a sound system of internal control;
- *implementation*–appointment of external support;
- *risk management process*–incremental phases of a six-stage iterative process;
- *identification of sources of risk*–internal and external.

Figure 2 provides an overview of the ERM corporate governance model, which includes feedback loops to allow for iterations at each stage, the rationale being that it is futile to continue the process if the foundation stages are found to be flawed as a result of subsequent research and review stages.

Figure 2. Risk and opportunity governance and management framework model

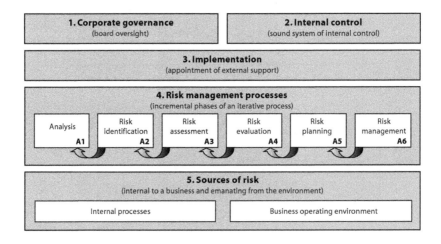

The ERM process is a six-stage iterative process, as illustrated in Figure 3.

Figure 3. Risk and opportunity management processes

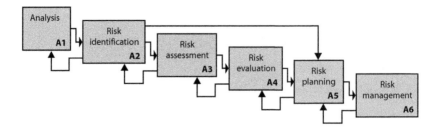

Each of the six risk management processes has inputs, outputs, controls, and mechanisms. The modes of data connectivity can be charted using the integrated definition for function modeling (IDEFO) process mapping technique, as illustrated in Figure 4.

Figure 4. Risk and opportunity management process control

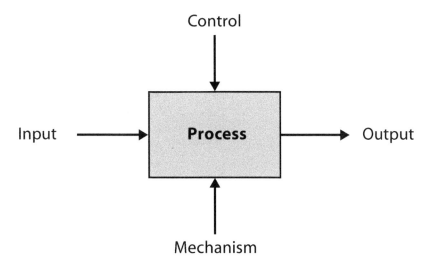

Sources of risk exist both internally and externally to the business (Figure 5) and interact to generate new risks. *Internal risk* has its origin within and may (potentially) be controlled by an organization. An example is financial risk, the exposure to adverse events that can adversely affect profitability and may trigger closure of a business.

External sources of risk are sources of risk that occur at subnational, national, regional, and global/international levels. These sources are largely exogenous to the insurer, such as demographic trends; however, some factors may be influenced by the insurer or its peers (e.g. regulation which addresses market and consumer issues). External sources of risk include the economic, natural/physical, political, legal and regulatory environments, market structures and conditions, legislation, and sociodemographic and cultural factors.

Figure 5. Internal and external sources of risk

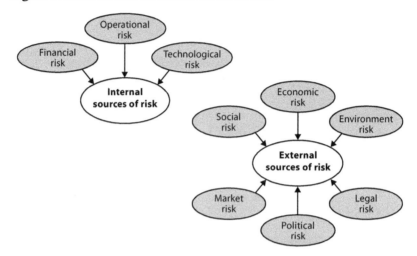

Elucidating a firm's risk appetite requires a consideration of "downside" and "upside" risks. Viewing risk appetite as the firm's **efficient risk frontier** is a useful way of helping participants to map out the upside and downside risks in order to develop a more robust, realistic view of the likely dimensions of their risk appetite. The risk and opportunity management (ROM) matrix approach in respect of a general insurance undertaking visualizes the "**risk-efficient frontier**" concept using graphics to help the board and senior management to develop an approach which is both coherent and internally consistent. This is shown in Figure 6.

Figure 6. Risk and opportunity management (ROM) matrix

		Risk				Opportunity		
Very likely	Low	Medium	High	High	High	High	Medium	Low
Likely	Low	Medium	High	High	High	High	Medium	Low
Unlikely	Low	Medium	Medium	Medium	Medium	Medium	Medium	Low
Very unlikely	Low	Low	Low	Low	Low	Low	Low	Low
	Negligible	Minor	Significant	Major	Major	Significant	Minor	Negligible
		Consequence				**Benefit**		

Probability

The emerging indicators and lessons for the future for each of the case study enterprises should also be considered. Risk and opportunity management involves a living organism (Figure 7). The processes and their feedback loops need to be constantly monitored and scrutinized.

Figure 7. Risk and opportunity management—a living organism

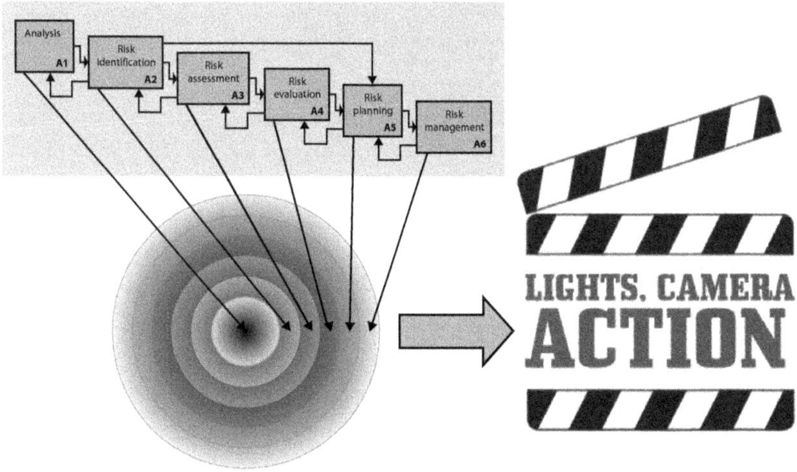

The ERM processes need to be sequential and iterative, with active feedback loops; otherwise, as in an onion, a rotten inner core will not lead to a sound onion fit for human consumption. In the ERM utopia, with your real-time risk dashboard to help with real-time decision-making it is vital that you have total confidence in each of the early warning indicators.

Case Studies

Case Study 1: American International Group (AIG)

The AIG story begins just short of 100 years ago in Asia. The history of AIG is impressive, and it was built to succeed. The company started life in Shanghai, founded by a keen businessman by the name of C. V. Star. Star had no knowledge of insurance; he did however have a keen eye for business opportunities. He grew AIG into a multinational insurer/broker that spanned multiple countries.

AIG experienced decent growth, but that all changed when Hank Greenberg took the helm. He turned AIG into one of the largest companies in the world. Was this all good? Greenberg instilled a culture in AIG of succeeding at any price, and he coined the rule of "15," which meant 15% growth in revenue, in profit, and in return on equity. The executive and all employees were encouraged to do whatever needed to be done to achieve these figures. In the process of growing AIG, Greenberg also produced numerous millionaires. Those who succeeded were rewarded very well, giving even more incentive to succeed.

Greenberg surrounded himself with a board that could help him. He selected board members himself, not to provide governance for the company but to connect the company to other organizations that could help AIG to grow. Most AIG board members were known personally to Greenberg before they were appointed. The board was therefore

unable/unwilling to perform the duties that a board should take of assessing and questioning the CEO and senior management until it was too late.

The AIG culture led to the first problem in early 2000. Two executives were convicted of colluding with Marsh & McLennan Companies (MMC) in insurance price fixing. This was the first victim of the AIG culture. But definitely not the last.

In 2005 New York State Attorney General Eliot Spitzer accused Greenberg of adjusting the company's accounting figures. Greenberg adjusted the figures somewhat to achieve his rule of 15 to satisfy analysts that AIG was still performing. He did this by manipulating reinsurance contracts through closely held reinsurance companies.

In September 2008, AIG was facing bankruptcy. Since 2005, AIG had become the poster boy for corporate governance; however, this was unfortunately too late. Its UK division had started to sell large amounts of credit default swaps (CDS) to various counterparties. CDSs allowed AIG to collect the "insurance" premium as long as the insured company did not default. Normally this was a great way of collecting money without having to set aside capital to cover the risk as these contracts were derivatives and in good times companies rarely defaulted. In 2008, AIG had an estimated CDS exposure of US$441 billion. AIG had treated CDSs as insurance in the sense that it assumed that all companies are independent, which in reality is not true. There is a correlation of failure among companies. When the credit crisis unfolded, AIG faced the threat of having its credit rating downgraded. It became apparent that it would not be able to cover the margins that would need to be paid to the CDS counterparties. The US government had to step in to bail out AIG to the tune of US$85 billion. This was just the first payment made by the US government.

Early warning indicators that could have been useful were:
- analysis, monitoring, and tracking of the corporate culture;
- a corporate ERM governance policy and its implementation;
- a corporate ethics policy and its implementation;
- reports by the CRO on ERM implementation and issues;
- strategic thinking on the business model (value chain, process);
- investigation of "stars" (e.g. business units, individuals);
- whistle-blowing reports, analysis, and tracking;
- internal audit reporting, training, and culture;
- risk incident reporting, training, and culture;
- management control of reports on all potentially material risks;
- business model systems and internal controls.

Lessons to be learned:
- A controlled corporate culture could have prevented employees from going too far. The culture at AIG was heavily focused on succeeding at any cost. Adjusting accounting figures and dealing illegally with insurance companies could have been avoided if the company had instituted and used an effective corporate ethics policy.
- A single business unit can bring down a whole organization. A chain is only as strong as its weakest link.
- Always consider all risks regardless of how unlikely they are to occur. Remember the black swan effect.
- Effective management controls could have prevented the disaster.
- Effective risk monitoring could have identified overexposure to certain risks.
- With the benefit of hindsight, the organization lost sight of its core business model, which was that of an insurance firm and not an investment bank.

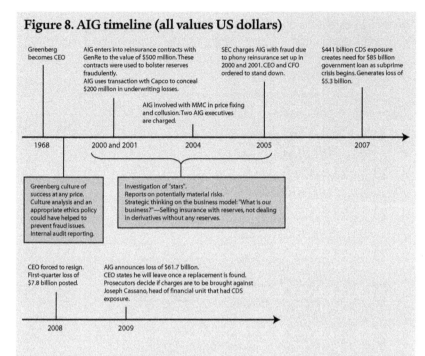

Figure 8. AIG timeline (all values US dollars)

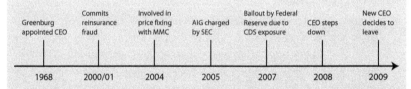

Figure 9. AIG summary timeline

Case Study 2: Long Term Capital Management (LTCM)

Strategic thinking about the business model could have prevented this disaster. LTCM provides a reminder of the notion that there is no such thing as a risk-free arbitrage. Because the arbitrage positions they were exploiting were small, the fund had to be leveraged many times in order to produce meaningful investment returns. The problem with liquidity is that it is never there when it is really needed.

Rigorous strategic analysis and understanding of the business model should precede development of technical business model systems and a resilient ERM implementation. LTCM was essentially a hedge fund founded in 1993 by John Meriwether. Its board of directors included Myron Scholes and Robert C. Merton, who shared the 1997 Nobel Memorial Prize in Economic Sciences. LTCM used complex mathematical models to identify relative value or convergence arbitrage trades which, for example, exploited small price differences between related securities such as US, Japanese, and European government bonds. Trading strategies made returns in excess of 40% in 1995 and 1996. However, LTCM's trading strategy relied on aggressive leverage to boost absolute performance—for example, a 1.0% per annum return on assets (actual earnings) leveraged at 25:1 would yield an apparent 25% per annum return.

Corporate culture and ethics need to be scrutinized to ensure that they deliver sufficient transparency and disclosure to stakeholders. In LTCM's case, this would have included ensuring that the providers of credit were able to assess whether its aggressive arbitrage strategy was aligned with their own risk appetite. It also should have included the client investors, who paid above average fees and were locked into an initial three-year relationship with LTCM. Transparency might have elicited intelligence to improve the robustness of the trading strategy and enable a different response on September 2, 1998. By this point LTCM had just US$400 million in capital. With assets still in excess of US$100 billion, this meant a leverage ratio of more than 250:1. LTCM's partners lost their own investment (US$1.9 billion), UBS lost US$700 million, and other investors lost US$1.8 billion.

LTCM failed because both its trading models and its risk management models failed to anticipate the extreme scenario of Russia's default on its government debt and the cycle of losses that followed. The announcement led to a global review of credit and sovereign risks. Panicked investors sold Japanese and European bonds to buy US Treasury bonds. The profits that were supposed to occur as the value of these bonds converged became huge losses as the value of the bonds diverged. LTCM lost US$550 million on August 21, 1998, and by the end of August the fund had lost US$1.85 billion in capital. With assets at US$1.26 billion, leverage had increased to 55:1.

Reliance on VaR-based models should have been subject to continuous scrutiny. In the event, the models did not foresee or provide for the extreme volatility and violence of the cycle of losses. Stress-testing also needs to be calibrated to the complexity and risk profile of the arbitrage. In this case it was inadequate; for example, the anticipated level of volatility of US$44 million was exceeded, with LTCM experiencing volatility of US$100 million and more. The company's 10-day VaR was US$320 million—compared to actual losses in August 1998 of over US$1,000 million.

Early warning indicators that could have been useful were:
- analysis, monitoring, and tracking of corporate culture;
- a corporate ERM governance policy and its implementation;
- a corporate ethics policy and its implementation;
- strategic thinking on the business model (value chain, process);
- a watch list of exposure to reputational loss (stakeholders, risks);
- investigation of "stars" (e.g. business units, individuals);
- whistle-blowing reports, analysis, and tracking;
- internal audit reporting, training, and culture;
- risk incident reporting, training, and culture;
- control by management of reports on all potentially material risks;
- business model systems and internal controls.

Lessons to be learned:
- An organization is only as strong as its weakest link.
- Strategic thinking about the business model could have prevented the disaster.
- VaR has proved to be unreliable as a measure of risk over long time periods or under abnormal market conditions. The danger posed by exceptional market shocks can be captured only by means of supplemental methodologies.
- The catastrophic losses were caused by systemic risks that LTCM had not foreseen in its business model. The failure of the hedge fund is a classic example of model risk in the financial services industry.
- LTCM provides a reminder of the notion that there is no such thing as a risk-free arbitrage. Because the arbitrage positions they were exploiting were small, the fund had to be leveraged many times in order to produce meaningful investment returns. The problem with liquidity is that it is never there when it is really needed.

- As LTCM's capital base grew, it felt pressured to invest that capital. As it had run out of good bond arbitrage bets, it turned to more aggressive trading strategies.
- LTCM failed because both its trading models and its risk management models failed to anticipate the cycle of losses that could occur during an extreme crisis when volatilities rose dramatically, correlations between markets and instruments became closer to 1, and liquidity dried up.
- Risk control at LTCM relied on a VaR model. However, the company's risk modeling was inappropriate and let it down.
- The theories of Merton and Scholes took a public beating. In its annual reports, Merrill Lynch observed that mathematical risk models "may provide a greater sense of security than warranted; therefore, reliance on these models should be limited."
- Effective management controls could have prevented the disaster.

Figure 10. LTCM timeline (all values US dollars)

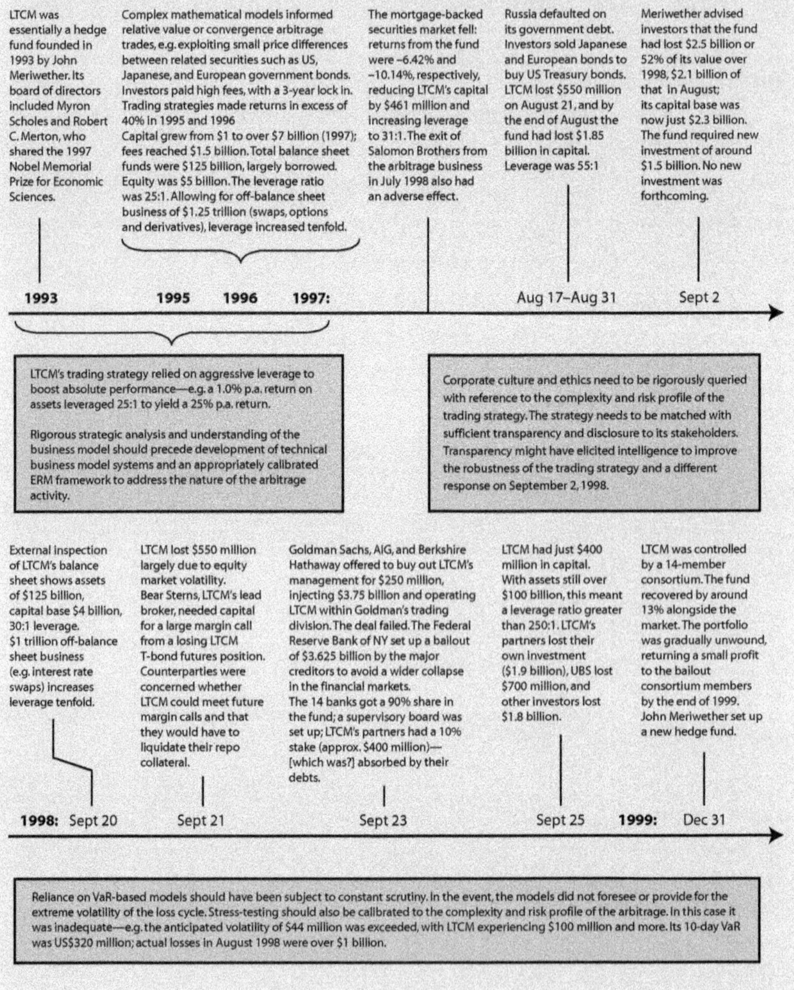

LTCM was essentially a hedge fund founded in 1993 by John Meriwether. Its board of directors included Myron Scholes and Robert C. Merton, who shared the 1997 Nobel Memorial Prize for Economic Sciences.

Complex mathematical models informed relative value or convergence arbitrage trades, e.g. exploiting small price differences between related securities such as US, Japanese, and European government bonds. Trading strategies made returns in excess of 40% in 1995 and 1996. Capital grew from $1 to over $7 billion (1997); fees reached $1.5 billion. Total balance sheet funds were $125 billion, largely borrowed. Equity was $5 billion. The leverage ratio was 25:1. Allowing for off-balance sheet business of $1.25 trillion (swaps, options and derivatives), leverage increased tenfold.

The mortgage-backed securities market fell: returns from the fund were −6.42% and −10.14%, respectively, reducing LTCM's capital by $461 million and increasing leverage to 31:1. The exit of Salomon Brothers from the arbitrage business in July 1998 also had an adverse effect.

Russia defaulted on its government debt. Investors sold Japanese and European bonds to buy US Treasury bonds. LTCM lost $550 million on August 21, and by the end of August the fund had lost $1.85 billion in capital. Leverage was 55:1.

Meriwether advised investors that the fund had lost $2.5 billion or 52% of its value over 1998, $2.1 billion of that in August; its capital base was now just $2.3 billion. The fund required new investment of around $1.5 billion. No new investment was forthcoming.

1993   **1995   1996   1997:**   Aug 17–Aug 31   Sept 2

LTCM's trading strategy relied on aggressive leverage to boost absolute performance—e.g. a 1.0% p.a. return on assets leveraged 25:1 to yield a 25% p.a. return.

Rigorous strategic analysis and understanding of the business model should precede development of technical business model systems and an appropriately calibrated ERM framework to address the nature of the arbitrage activity.

Corporate culture and ethics need to be rigorously queried with reference to the complexity and risk profile of the trading strategy. The strategy needs to be matched with sufficient transparency and disclosure to its stakeholders. Transparency might have elicited intelligence to improve the robustness of the trading strategy and a different response on September 2, 1998.

External inspection of LTCM's balance sheet shows assets of $125 billion, capital base $4 billion, 30:1 leverage. $1 trillion off-balance sheet business (e.g. interest rate swaps) increases leverage tenfold.

LTCM lost $550 million largely due to equity market volatility. Bear Sterns, LTCM's lead broker, needed capital for a large margin call from a losing LTCM T-bond futures position. Counterparties were concerned whether LTCM could meet future margin calls and that they would have to liquidate their repo collateral.

Goldman Sachs, AIG, and Berkshire Hathaway offered to buy out LTCM's management for $250 million, injecting $3.75 billion and operating LTCM within Goldman's trading division. The deal failed. The Federal Reserve Bank of NY set up a bailout of $3.625 billion by the major creditors to avoid a wider collapse in the financial markets. The 14 banks got a 90% share in the fund; a supervisory board was set up; LTCM's partners had a 10% stake (approx. $400 million)— [which was?] absorbed by their debts.

LTCM had just $400 million in capital. With assets still over $100 billion, this meant a leverage ratio greater than 250:1. LTCM's partners lost their own investment ($1.9 billion), UBS lost $700 million, and other investors lost $1.8 billion.

LTCM was controlled by a 14-member consortium. The fund recovered by around 13% alongside the market. The portfolio was gradually unwound, returning a small profit to the bailout consortium members by the end of 1999. John Meriwether set up a new hedge fund.

1998: Sept 20   Sept 21   Sept 23   Sept 25   **1999:** Dec 31

Reliance on VaR-based models should have been subject to constant scrutiny. In the event, the models did not foresee or provide for the extreme volatility of the loss cycle. Stress-testing should also be calibrated to the complexity and risk profile of the arbitrage. In this case it was inadequate—e.g. the anticipated volatility of $44 million was exceeded, with LTCM experiencing $100 million and more. Its 10-day VaR was US$320 million; actual losses in August 1998 were over $1 billion.

Figure 11. LTCM summary timeline (all values US dollars)

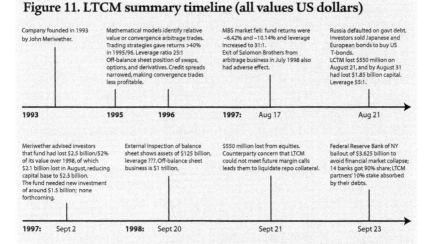

Case Study 3: Union Carbide India Ltd's Bhopal Plant

The severity of the accident at Bhopal in Madhya Pradesh state, India, makes it the worst recorded in the chemical industry. At midnight on December 2, 1984, a relief valve on a storage tank containing highly toxic methyl isocyanate (MIC) lifted, releasing a toxic plume of gas that drifted on to nearby housing, exposing more than 500,000 residents. Estimates of the death toll vary. The official immediate death toll was 2,259, and the government of Madhya Pradesh has confirmed a total of 3,787 deaths related to the gas release. Other government agencies estimate 15,000 deaths. Others estimate that 8,000 to 10,000 died within 72 hours, and that 25,000 have since died from gas-related diseases. 40,000 more were permanently disabled, maimed, or rendered subject to numerous grave illnesses.

Strategic thinking about the business model might have halted backward integration and inappropriate use of the plant. If Union Carbide India Ltd (UCIL) had analyzed the proposed changes in its business model, it might have decided not to proceed with backward integration involving the processing of raw materials, production of intermediate compounds, and manufacture of the final Sevin pesticide—certainly not without a robust ERM implementation. It might thus have avoided the unacceptable level of risk exposure that arose from attempting to maintain production while decommissioning processes and safety equipment.

Strategic thinking about the business model should take the broadest view of the firm's value chain and apply the ERM framework across the chain. UCIL should have examined its entire value chain and identified the risks attached to poor safety equipment and standards; it should have prioritized the provision and maintenance of specific plant (flare system, vent gas system, operative refrigeration with coolant) and identified areas where there was insufficient knowledge within the organization to manage certain processes—for example, the risk and management of runaway reactions in a gas storage tank.

Corporate culture needs to encourage and promote adherence to risk management. UCIL, some suggest, is an example of the application by multinational corporations of double standards in their operations in developing countries. This engendered a corporate culture within the subsidiary that led to degraded safety procedures and equipment.

Corporate culture and ethics need to be scrutinized and addressed to see that they ensure sufficient transparency and disclosure to stakeholders. The Bhopal facility was operating with safety equipment and procedures far inferior to its sister plant in the United States. The local government wanted to retain UCIL as a large employer and so was hesitant to insist on safety and pollution controls despite its awareness of the poor standards at the plant. UCIL changed the plant's activities from a relatively lower-risk chemical process to manufacture the final pesticide product to the more hazardous and complex backward integration process described above. Full consultation on the evolving business model would have enabled the local authority to consider the implications for its (and its residents) risk appetite. The UCIL plant was operating outside of its zoning requirements for light industry in a residential area when the incident occurred.

Effective internal controls and risk incident reporting should have alerted the management to breaches in safety equipment and standards at the plant in critical equipment—for example the vent gas system (VGS) and the potential runaway reaction in the storage tank. Failings in technical measures at the plant included:

- the flare system, which was a critical element of the plant's protection system (UCIL did not recognize this), had been out of commission for three months;
- hazards from runaway reactions in a chemical reactor are understood, but occurrences in storage tanks had received little research;

- the ingress of water caused an exothermic reaction with the process fluid (the exact point of ingress is uncertain, though poor modification/ maintenance practices may have contributed);
- decommissioning of the refrigeration system (a plant modification) contributed to the accident as without this system the temperature in the tank was higher than the design temperature of 0°C.

The absence of risk planning and management can serve to increase the severity and impact of a major incident. UCIL had not led consultation with the local authority and public services to plan, scenario-test, and implement a plan to manage a major incident. When at around 1.00 a.m. on December 3 a safety valve gave way, sending a plume of MIC gas into the early morning air, an estimated 3,800 people died immediately, many in the poor slum quarters near the plant. No siren was sounded to warn residents, and the public services, including the hospitals, had no information on what the gas was or what it effects were.

Early warning indicators that could have been useful:
- analysis, monitoring, and tracking of corporate culture;
- a corporate ERM governance policy and its implementation;
- a corporate ethics policy and its implementation;
- strategic thinking on the business model (value chain, process);
- a watch list of exposure to reputational loss (stakeholders, risks);
- investigation of "stars" (e.g. business units, individuals);
- whistle-blowing reports, analysis, and tracking;
- internal audit reporting, training, and culture;
- risk incident reporting, training, and culture;
- control by management of reports on all potentially material risks;
- use of business model systems and internal controls.

Lessons to be learned:
- An organization is only as strong as its weakest link.
- Reputational damage travels swiftly and is difficult to reverse.
- Strategic thinking about the business model could have prevented the disaster.

- A corporate ethics policy based on best practice could have prevented the disaster.
- Effective management controls could have prevented the disaster.
- The court proceedings revealed that the management's cost-cutting measures had effectively disabled safety procedures essential to the prevention of the disaster and to alerting employees of such disasters.
- The severity and impact of the event were made worse by the lack of safety standards and effective containment measures. The physical manifestations of these failures included unreliable monitoring equipment, inoperative safety equipment, unsuitable and inadequate gas suppression equipment, and alarm systems which failed.
- On-going litigation continues to haunt Dow Chemical, which subsequently took over Union Carbide, despite its denial of responsibility for the disaster.
- A risk event at a small foreign subsidiary can bring down the entire enterprise. Risk management at all levels should recognize that the potential for catastrophes always exists and that their impact can be both large-scale and a long-term.
- We can never predict events like Bhopal, but an enterprise should accept that the risk always remains of a catastrophic disaster. The foundation of a risk management strategy needs to be strong in its fundamentals, such as ensuring adherence to appropriate safety standards.

Figure 12. Union Carbide Timeline

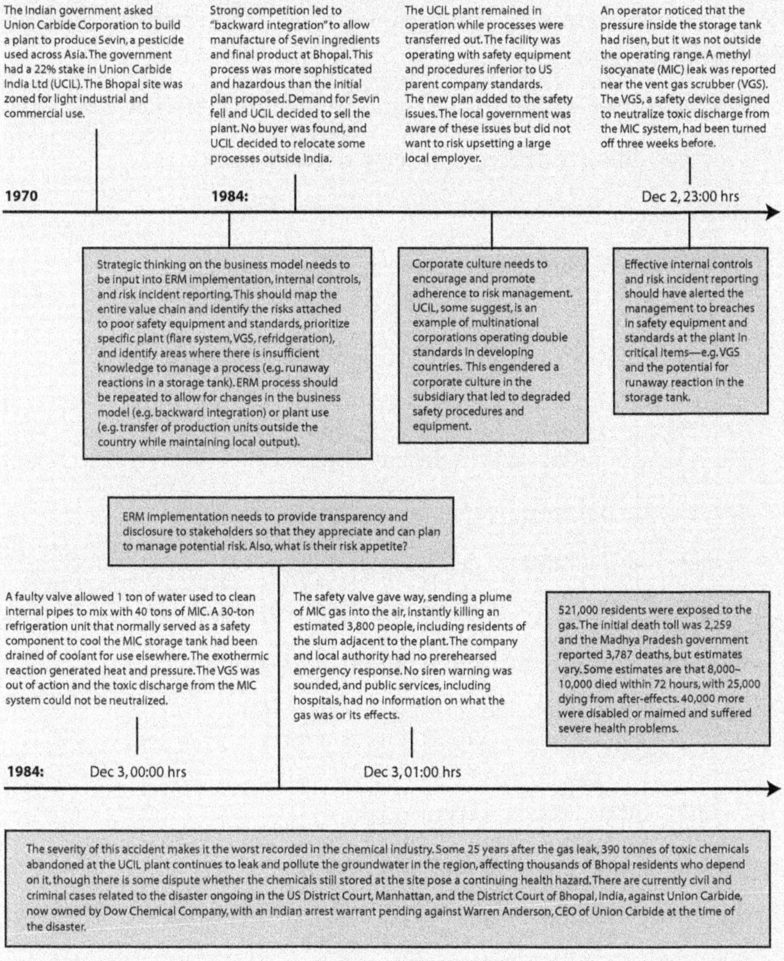

The Indian government asked Union Carbide Corporation to build a plant to produce Sevin, a pesticide used across Asia. The government had a 22% stake in Union Carbide India Ltd (UCIL). The Bhopal site was zoned for light industrial and commercial use.

Strong competition led to "backward integration" to allow manufacture of Sevin ingredients and final product at Bhopal. This process was more sophisticated and hazardous than the initial plan proposed. Demand for Sevin fell and UCIL decided to sell the plant. No buyer was found, and UCIL decided to relocate some processes outside India.

The UCIL plant remained in operation while processes were transferred out. The facility was operating with safety equipment and procedures inferior to US parent company standards. The new plan added to the safety issues. The local government was aware of these issues but did not want to risk upsetting a large local employer.

An operator noticed that the pressure inside the storage tank had risen, but it was not outside the operating range. A methyl isocyanate (MIC) leak was reported near the vent gas scrubber (VGS). The VGS, a safety device designed to neutralize toxic discharge from the MIC system, had been turned off three weeks before.

1970   **1984:**   **Dec 2, 23:00 hrs**

Strategic thinking on the business model needs to be input into ERM implementation, internal controls, and risk incident reporting. This should map the entire value chain and identify the risks attached to poor safety equipment and standards, prioritize specific plant (flare system, VGS, refridgeration), and identify areas where there is insufficient knowledge to manage a process (e.g. runaway reactions in a storage tank). ERM process should be repeated to allow for changes in the business model (e.g. backward integration) or plant use (e.g. transfer of production units outside the country while maintaining local output).

Corporate culture needs to encourage and promote adherence to risk management. UCIL, some suggest, is an example of multinational corporations operating double standards in developing countries. This engendered a corporate culture in the subsidiary that led to degraded safety procedures and equipment.

Effective internal controls and risk incident reporting should have alerted the management to breaches in safety equipment and standards at the plant in critical items—e.g. VGS and the potential for runaway reaction in the storage tank.

ERM implementation needs to provide transparency and disclosure to stakeholders so that they appreciate and can plan to manage potential risk. Also, what is their risk appetite?

A faulty valve allowed 1 ton of water used to clean internal pipes to mix with 40 tons of MIC. A 30-ton refrigeration unit that normally served as a safety component to cool the MIC storage tank had been drained of coolant for use elsewhere. The exothermic reaction generated heat and pressure. The VGS was out of action and the toxic discharge from the MIC system could not be neutralized.

The safety valve gave way, sending a plume of MIC gas into the air, instantly killing an estimated 3,800 people, including residents of the slum adjacent to the plant. The company and local authority had no prerehearsed emergency response. No siren warning was sounded, and public services, including hospitals, had no information on what the gas was or its effects.

521,000 residents were exposed to the gas. The initial death toll was 2,259 and the Madhya Pradesh government reported 3,787 deaths, but estimates vary. Some estimates are that 8,000–10,000 died within 72 hours, with 25,000 dying from after-effects. 40,000 more were disabled or maimed and suffered severe health problems.

1984:   **Dec 3, 00:00 hrs**   **Dec 3, 01:00 hrs**

The severity of this accident makes it the worst recorded in the chemical industry. Some 25 years after the gas leak, 390 tonnes of toxic chemicals abandoned at the UCIL plant continues to leak and pollute the groundwater in the region, affecting thousands of Bhopal residents who depend on it, though there is some dispute whether the chemicals still stored at the site pose a continuing health hazard. There are currently civil and criminal cases related to the disaster ongoing in the US District Court, Manhattan, and the District Court of Bhopal, India, against Union Carbide, now owned by Dow Chemical Company, with an Indian arrest warrant pending against Warren Anderson, CEO of Union Carbide at the time of the disaster.

Conclusions from the Case Studies

The principal research conclusions from the case studies are summarized below.

1. Need for an appropriate, robust, and applied ERM framework model:

- six-stage iterative process model with feedback loops;
- corporate governance essential—led from the top;
- internal systems and controls essential;
- awareness of internal and external sources of risk;
- upside and downside—risk and opportunity management.

2. ERM process model that might have helped:

- effective corporate governance, systems, and controls;
- management awareness of business model and value chains;
- corporate culture assessment—regulatory review;
- scenario planning—stress-testing extreme conditions;
- opportunity management of upside potential.

3. Timelines for unexpected events:

- the future is largely unpredictable;
- the future unfolds rapidly for adverse risk incidents;
- the historical perspective is often post-rationalized;
- timelines are rarely within the management's control;
- timely service recovery requires an agile management team.

4. Emerging risk from unexpected events:

- the future is not what it used to be;

- black swans and the fallacy of inductive logic;
- the trap of false enthusiasm;
- emerging risks—pro-activity versus re-activity;
- emerging risks with the benefit of hindsight.

5. Lessons to be learned:
- lessons from internal risk incident reviews;
- lessons from historical reviews and post-mortems;
- lessons from management role-play exercises;
- lessons from scenario planning—team decisions;
- lessons from survival training—team decisions.

6. Early warning indicators that might have helped:
- every early warning indicator should be actionable;
- real-time early warning indicator dashboards;
- Solvency II "use test"—in the driving seat;
- indicator dashboard as a tool for management action;
- less can be more....

7. Corporate governance that might have helped:
- early warning indicators for the governing body;
- pictures and storyboards—the "elevator" test;
- Solvency II "use test"—cannot be delegated;
- not just a box-ticking exercise;
- no excuses for not understanding the business model.

More Info

General:

Orros, George C. "ERM for emerging risks in general insurance." GIRO Conference and Exhibition, Newport, UK, October 12–15, 2010. Online at: tinyurl.com/k5fdmfe

Orros, George C. "ERM for emerging risks in general insurance." Momentum Conference, November 30–December 2, 2011. Online at: tinyurl.com/lz3jpvj

Case Study 1—AIG (American International Group):

Davidson, Adam. "How AIG fell apart." *Reuters* (September 18, 2008). Online at: tinyurl.com/br4u6ue

Farrell, Greg. "Prosecutors to decide whether to charge former AIG executive." *Financial Times* (September 12, 2009). Online at: tinyurl.com/ktg8x6p

Felsted, Andrea, and Kate Burgess. "AIG forms keystone of financial system." *Financial Times* (September 16, 2008). Online at: tinyurl.com/myc8lcs

SEC. "AIG to pay $800 million to settle securities fraud charges by SEC." February 9, 2006. Online at: www.sec.gov/news/press/2006-19.htm

Valdmanis, Thor, Adam Shell and Elliot Blair Smith. "Marsh & McLennan accused of price fixing, collusion." *USA Today* (October 15, 2004). Online at: tinyurl.com/4t3p2

Williams Walsh, Mary. "Risky trading wasn't just on the fringe at A.I.G." *New York Times* (January 31, 2010). Online at: www.nytimes.com/2010/02/01/business/01swaps.html

Case Study 2—LTCM (Long Term Capital Management):

Crouhy, Michel, Dan Galai, and Robert Mark. *The Essentials of Risk Management*. New York: McGraw-Hill, 2006.

Drobny, Steven. *Inside the House of Money: Top Hedge Fund Traders on Profiting in the Global Markets*. Hoboken, NJ: Wiley, 2006.

Lam, James. *Enterprise Risk Management: From Incentives to Controls.* Hoboken, NJ: Wiley, 2003.

McNeil, Alexander J., Rüdiger Frey, and Paul Embrechts. *Quantitative Risk Management: Concepts, Tools, Techniques.* Princeton, NJ: Princeton University Press, 2005.

Wikipedia on LTCM: en.wikipedia.org/wiki/LTCM

Case Study 3—Union Carbide:

Associated Press. "Seven found guilty of Bhopal gas tragedy." *Independent* (June 7, 2010). Online at: tinyurl.com/24rfh6t

Broughton, Edward. "The Bhopal disaster and its aftermath: A review." *Environmental Health* 4:6 (May 10, 2005). Online at: dx.doi.org/10.1186/1476-069X-4-6

Lam (2003)—see under Case Study 2.

Skipper, Harold D., and W. Jean Kwon. *Risk Management and Insurance: Perspectives in a Global Economy.* Malden, MA: Blackwell Publishing, 2007.

Wikipedia on Union Carbide: en.wikipedia.org/wiki/Union_Carbide

ERM, Best's Ratings, and the Financial Crisis

by Gene C. Lai

This Chapter Covers

- The objective of ERM should be to maximize the wealth of all stakeholders, including stockholders, policy-holders, creditors, and employees.

- To have a successful ERM process, a company needs to have an effective risk culture, and have the support of the CEO and other executive officers, such as the CRO or CFO.

- The ERM process should include capital modeling tools, and hold high-quality and sufficient capital.

- An effective ERM will have a positive impact, not only on the best capital adequacy ratio (BCAR) but also on Best's overall ratings.

- In addition to the traditional ERM, and recent improvements such as dynamic hedging models, an effective ERM needs to consider the systemic risks that made some insurance companies insolvent in the recent financial crisis.

Introduction

The recent financial crisis has raised some questions, such as why enterprise risk management (ERM) was not able to prevent some large insurance companies from either becoming insolvent (for example, AIG) or from suffering large losses of their market value (for example, Lincoln National), and whether rating agencies properly perform their jobs.[1] It is critical that insurance companies have effective ERM programs, and that rating agencies provide adequate ratings to protect insurance companies from bankruptcy. Initially, many insurance companies adopt ERM because rating agencies consider ERM as part of their rating. Adopting ERM for the sole purpose of fulfilling the requirements of a rating agency may not be the best practice. A recent survey conducted by Towers Perrin showed that 32% of companies name identifying and quantifying risk as their main purpose. We believe these companies are moving in the right direction, but more improvements to the current ERM process are needed.

Effective ERM

To have an effective ERM, a company needs to have an effective risk culture. To achieve an effective risk culture, a company needs to start from the chief executive officer (CEO) and other senior executive officers (including the chief financial officer (CFO) and/or the chief risk officer (CRO)).

ERM usually involves a process that identifies and assesses risks, determines a response strategy and techniques, and implements and monitors the risk-management program for the enterprise. The objective of an ERM program is to maximize the wealth of the stakeholders—including stockholders, policy-holders, creditors, and employees—sustainably over the long term. It should be noted that wealth maximization is not equivalent to risk minimization. Risk and return are trade-offs. Insurance companies need first to establish their risk tolerance level and minimize unnecessary risk.

Some major categories of risk are credit risk, market risk, underwriting risk, operational risk, and strategic risk. Detailed items for each category of risk can be found in one of Best's articles.[2] In terms of credit risk, insurance companies should pay special attention to counterparty risk if they hold credit default swaps (CDSs). The recent collapse of AIG provides a good lesson for insurance companies that do not know the counterparty risk.

As a result of recent events such as September 11, 2001, the financial crisis which started in 2008, and major hurricanes in 2004, 2005, and 2012 (including Katrina, Rita, Wilma, and Sandy), longevity issues have increased the risk profile of insurance companies. Insurance companies have to take action to deal with the increased uncertainty and volatility that they face. In addition, the regulatory changes regarding EU Solvency II and principles-based requirements have also resulted in improvements to traditional risk management programs. Recent developments in ERM include catastrophe modeling, dynamic hedging modeling, and an enterprise-wide view of risk for insurance companies. Catastrophe modeling aims to deal with the rapid escalation of natural disasters caused by global warming, because it has been more difficult to predict catastrophic events. While the retirement of the baby-boomer generation presents opportunities for insurance companies to manage retirement savings, it also creates capital market-based risk. Insurance companies have developed some products that guarantee certain returns on the invested assets. The guarantees create additional risks related to capital market performance. To reduce the risk of the guarantees, insurance companies have developed and implemented sophisticated hedging models to protect both the policy holders and these companies against adverse movements in the capital markets. The recent financial crisis has shown that the hedging programs are far from perfect. Many insurance companies have suffered from rating downgrades and potential bankruptcy. The new emphasis on ERM today is a heuristic approach, rather than a silo approach. Not only the risk of an individual unit, but also the risk correlations among the units, are critical to the success of ERM. More importantly, ERM today should pay more attention to systemic risk, which can be defined as the risk of collapse of an entire financial system or capital market. One reason for the recent failure of the financial systems is that ERM does not consider the systemic risk.

ERM, BCAR, and AM Best Ratings

There are different rating agencies that rate insurance companies. Among them, AM Best is deemed as one of the most important. This chapter therefore focuses on the relationship between ERM and AM Best ratings. AM Best expects each insurance company to customize its ERM process to their integrated risk profile and risk management needs in order to maintain acceptable ratings. The ERM process should include capital modeling tools (such as dynamic financial analysis) to maintain appropriate capital. The process also needs to include a discussion of the impact of the company's ERM on its rating in its annual meetings.

The objective of AM Best's rating system is to "provide an opinion of an insurer's financial strength, and ability to meet ongoing obligations to policyholders." One of the most important factors of Best's rating is balance sheet strength. Best uses the BCAR to proxy balance sheet strength. BCAR is defined as the ratio of adjusted surplus to net required capital (NRC). The main components of adjusted surplus are reported surplus, equity adjustments, debt adjustments, and other adjustments. NRC includes fixed-income securities, equity securities, interest rate, credit risk, loss and loss-adjustment-expense reserves, net written premiums, and off-balance-sheet items. The BCAR formula also contains an adjustment for covariance, reflecting the correlation between individual components. BCAR is similar to the calculation of the National Association of Insurance Commissioners' (NAIC's) risk-based capital, but BCAR includes some important risk factors that are not considered by the NAIC's risk-based capital. BCAR can make adjustments to respond to various market issues such as rate changes, the stage of underwriting cycles, and reinsurance. It should be noted that more than two-thirds of an insurance company's gross capital requirements of BCAR comes from the company's loss reserve and net premiums written. Less than one-third of the gross capital requirements comes from investment risk, interest risk, and credit risk. After Best calculates a company's initial BCAR, it performs various sensitivity tests including the catastrophe and terrorism stress tests.

While BCAR is a critical quantitative model to measure financial strength and serve as a consistent baseline for Best ratings, it is not the sole basis for determining the final ratings. A corporate culture of risk awareness and accountability in daily operations, operating performance, business profile, and the quality of capital are also very important considerations for Best's ratings. ERM has an impact on a company's financial strength, operating performance (such as relative earnings and loss-ratio volatility), business profile (for example, catastrophe and terrorism risk exposures), and the quality of capital. Thus, an effective ERM has an important impact on the Best rating. An insurance company with a strong ERM can be allowed to lower its BCAR, compared with another company with a relatively weak ERM. It is even possible that an insurance company can keep its BCAR lower than the guideline level, on a case-by-case basis, and vice versa.

ERM and the Financial Crisis

This section does not intend to examine the causes of the recent financial crisis, but to discuss whether an effective ERM can mitigate the negative impact of the financial crisis on insurance companies. In the insurance industry, AIG received US$182 billion in bailout funding and was 80% owned by the US government.[3] Lincoln National , among other insurance companies, sought aid from the government. Why did ERM fail to prevent these companies from near collapse? Here are some possible answers. First, even though the concept of ERM has been popular for more than 10 years, insurance companies had not very seriously implemented ERM until recently. The current process is not perfect; while it considers the correlations among individual risks, it fails to consider the systemic risk facing the whole financial system, and the counterparty risk of derivative securities. To prevent future failures, the ERM approach needs to recognize that the solvency approach may not be appropriate in a financial crisis environment. Insurance companies need to have more capital than BCAR requires, because additional capital is difficult to obtain during a financial crisis. Second, CROs need to resist the temptation to sell complex products without really understanding the consequences of selling those products. The CDSs of AIG are an example. Finally, insurance companies should focus on their core business—underwriting business—rather than investing in exotic derivatives.

Case Study

ERM and the Ratings of USAA and Its Subsidiaries

In December 2008, AM Best confirmed it had given USAA and its subsidiaries (hereafter USAA) the financial strength rating (FSR) of A++ (superior) rating, issuer credit rating (ICR) of "aaa," and the debt rating of "aaa." The ratings reflect "USAA's superior capitalization and strong operating results through focused business and financial strategy." Diversified sources of earnings, capital accumulation, and strong ERM are also key factors for superior ratings. In addition, good catastrophe management, a sound reinsurance program to preserve the finance capital, and a conservative investment strategy were mentioned. The USAA case demonstrates that Best's ratings reflect the effectiveness of USAA's ERM.

Conclusion

ERM has become more and more important in recent years. The recent financial crisis makes ERM even more critical to the success and survival of enterprises, especially insurance companies. For example, the Financial Stability Oversight Council is reviewing Prudential Financial Inc. and may label Prudential "systemically important." To have a successful ERM process, a company needs to have support from the CEO and other executive officers such as the CRO or CFO. The ERM process should include capital modeling tools, and hold sufficient high-quality capital. An effective ERM will have a positive impact not only on the BCAR but also on Best's overall ratings. In addition to traditional ERM, and recent improvements such as dynamic hedging models, an effective ERM needs to consider the systemic risks that made many insurance companies insolvent in the recent financial crisis.

More Info

Book:
Moeller, Robert. *COSO Enterprise Risk Management: Understanding the New Integrated ERM Framework*. Hoboken, NJ: Wiley, 2007.

Articles:
Kenealy, Bill. "Sifting through the ashes to assess ERM's value." *Insurance Networking News* (January 7, 2009). Online at: tinyurl.com/5ukt6zu

Mueller, Hubert, Eric Simpson, and Edward Easop. "The best of ERM." *Emphasis* 2008/3: 6–9. Online at: tinyurl.com/6b9m989

Reports:
AM Best. "Risk management and the rating process for insurance companies." Methodology. January 25, 2008. Online at: www.ambest.com/ratings/methodology/riskmanagement.pdf

Mosher, Matthew C. "A.M. Best comments on enterprise risk management and capital models." Special Report. AM Best, February 2006. Online at: www.ambest.com/ratings/methodology/enterpriserisk.pdf

Website:
A collection of essays from the Society of Actuaries, *Risk Management: The Current Financial Crisis, Lessons Learned and Future Implications:* www.soa.org/library/essays/rm-essay-2008-toc.aspx

1 In addition, Prudential Financial Inc. and Hartford Financial Services Group Inc. reported losses of more than US$1 billion in the second half of 2008.

2 See AM Best (2008).

3 The US$182 billion bailout turned out to be profitable for the US government.

Issues in Issuing Insurance-Linked Securities

by Morton Lane

This Chapter Covers

The checklist of considerations for insurers planning to issue insurance-linked securities (ILS) into the capital markets includes the following:

- Identify risk concentrations.
- Quantify the loss consequence of such concentrations.
- Design offsetting structure to transfer risks to capital markets with the help of agents.
- Engage a placement agent or investment banker—essential to fruitful design.
- Engage a risk modeling firm—essential to fruitful design.
- Decide on denomination of loss measures: indemnity or index.
- Choose SPV location and attendant experts in those locations.
- Review structure, design, price, and alternatives to ensure the ILS suitability.
- Execute.

Introduction

The first insurance-linked security (ILS) was conceived in 1992, three months before Hurricane Andrew. However, perhaps to the chagrin of the potential issuer, AIG, the deal was not consummated. Had it been, the issuer would have collected for both Hurricane Andrew and the Northridge earthquake of 1994. The first executed ILS took place two years later, but it and some subsequent issues were relatively small in size. Two years after that, the first sizable issue of a catastrophe ILS (usually referred to as "Cat ILS") heralded the beginning of the modern era. The cedant was the United Services Automobile Association (USAA), the placement agent was Goldman Sachs, and the issue size was US$500 million.

Since that beginning the market has steadily expanded to the undisputed advantage of investors and issuers alike. Almost US$45 billion in risk has been transferred from issuers of ILS to the capital markets (of which US$40 billion is Cat). Furthermore, every time there is another catastrophe, the revealed utility of ILS to cedants leads to increased adoption by traditional risk transferees in the insurance market. To date, issuance has been consummated by insureds (e.g. Tokyo Disneyland, Universal Studios), insurance companies (e.g. USAA, Hartford), reinsurers (e.g. Swiss Re, Munich Re), retrocessionaires (e.g. Montpelier Re, PXRE), official institutions (e.g. IBRD), and sovereigns (e.g. Mexico, North Carolina).

While each different type of issuer has particular needs, many elements of issuance are common to each. Our purpose here is to list the elements to consider when issuing ILS. These elements, listed by importance, are: risk concentration, effect on the overall portfolio of the ILS risk, the investment banker, the risk-modeling agency, denomination, choice of additional agents, the structure of the bond, and the law firm, as well as other factors. We discuss each element below.

The Important Elements of ILS Issuance

Risk Concentration

The first item on any issuer's checklist must be to identify the need to transfer risk. This means being able to describe and quantify exposures and the resulting concentrations. The concentrations in the exposures are where protection is needed. It is no accident that the biggest such concentration in many portfolios are wind events in the US. The US home-owners market is the biggest in the world. Scattered wind storms are not the concern; rather it is the concentrated devastation from a major hurricane. Such events generate huge numbers of claims for insurers with attendant large losses. But identification is not enough in itself.

Effect of ILS Risk on the Overall Portfolio

The second essential element is to be able to quantify the concentration exposure and the effect the concentration has on the overall portfolio.

This means employing a risk quantifying model. This can be done by a DFA [Dynamic Financial Analysis] analysis or some other portfolio analysis techniques, such as optimization. Now, such analysis is not just essential for issuers of ILS, it is a requirement of any purchaser of protection whether in the traditional reinsurance market or the capital markets. It also ought to be an essential ingredient in constructing an underwriting portfolio, whether or not one is buying protection. Thus, for most issuers part of the analysis is already in place. That will be especially true if the coverage for which protection is sought is an "indemnity" protection. Traditional reinsurance is by definition indemnity-based, and it means that the protector will protect the cedant for the exact amount of loss (or at least that part of the loss contracted for) that the cedant itself suffers.

In many traditional cases brokers will be partly familiar with the exposures and portfolio of the cedant. As a result the broker comes with products that are: available in the traditional market; and fit with the broker's perception of the cedant's needs. They will also present an analysis to fit. There is nothing wrong with this, but it is a model of behavior that has to be amended in interacting with capital markets. Cedants must take more initiative themselves in identifying the protection they need, rather than being reactive to broker's pitches. This should not be misunderstood. Brokers do provide valuable information about what is available in the market and what is the likely cost. However, simply identifying unattainable protection desires without knowing what is possible and at what price is as undesirable as simply reacting to whichever broker knocks on the door.

The Investment Banker

The point to start at is to identify your own perceived needs and then to engage a placement agent to effect those needs, as best is practical, in the chosen market. If the risk is to be placed in the capital market, that means that the third important choice for an issuer is the choice of investment banker. Well-known names such as Goldman Sachs and BNP Paribas operate in the ILS market, as do reinsurer capital market subsidiaries such as Swiss Re Capital Markets and Aon Benfield Securities. These and several other names come with their own skill sets and investor bases. They all also have different fee schedules. New issuers might well want to place investment bankers in competition (sometimes referred to as a beauty parade) before making their choice. They will be looking for cost differences, experience, market insight, and investor base—who can do the best job of helping to structure and distribute the securities. Often it is the case that two or more managers are chosen: one to lead, the others to co-manage.

The Risk-Modeling Agency

Having settled on an investment bank, the next important choice is the risk-modeling agency. Three firms share the bulk of the market: AIR Worldwide, RMS, and EQECAT. Investors are familiar with these firms, and while others are not excluded (indeed, Swiss Re and others have offered their own risk analysis to investors), investor comfort presently resides with these three firms. Also, each has its own approaches and its own strengths. It is best to choose the firm whose strengths most closely align with the peril against which protection is sought.

In the choice of either investment banker or risk modeler it is best not to be "penny wise and pound foolish." The investor will react to sloppy work, and it will cost the issuer to overcome unknowns or questionable work.

Denomination

The fifth important decision is how the protection is to be denominated. Indemnity cover is what most cedants want, but it is not most popular with investors. There is a feeling that there is an asymmetry of information between issuer and investor. The issuer knows the whole book; the investor does not. The investor could be taken advantage of, i.e., "selected against." Obviously this has echoes in the recent consternation about adverse selection of mortgages in the CDO market, but it is an issue that insurers have dealt with for centuries. If indemnity is the way in which losses are to be denominated, then most investors will require an "alignment of interest." In other words, the issuer must be alongside for part of the risk. As a rule, the higher the alignment retained by the issuer, the greater is the investor comfort. In ILS a 10% share is common, and 20% and 50% are frequently seen, as is 5%, but the latter does not have a good record. Moreover, the alignment should be permanent for the life of the ILS. Investors will not take kindly to an issuer who starts with a 10% alignment and then retrocedes it away. If the issuer does retrocede his share, for whatever good reason, the investor will want to be protected as well for the same good reason. At least the investor should have that option.

The other, much more common way to assure that the investor is not selected against is to base the loss on an index of loss or equivalent. To provide a specific example, if an earthquake risk is denominated on the Richter scale (the bigger the reading, the bigger the loss payment), it is hard to argue that the issuer has any more information than the investor—certainly he cannot select the exact reading. Independent scientific measuring stations will do that. Furthermore, the issuer will have engaged an independent risk modeler to assess the nature of the risk. Similar arguments apply to other indices—industry loss, wind speed, temperature, etc. Indeed, these days very sophisticated loss models can be built, archived on a computer, and used to calculate investor loss. These models can be constructed and weighted in such a way as to closely replicate cedant portfolios without having the perceived risk of indemnity cover. Any index solution will mean that the cedant will not have its loss exactly recompensed. For that he must gauge whether the benefit in investor acceptance is worth it.

Choice of Additional Agents

Beyond the choice of protection needs and appropriate selection of the most important agents, a host of smaller agent choices must be made. Which domicile should be used for the issuing special purpose vehicle (SPV)? Which manager should run the SPV? Who is the trustee and investment manager, the accountant, and the indenture agent? In dollar terms these decisions do not appear important, but sloppy choice here can have important consequences. In recent years the phrase "brain-dead SPV manager" has entered the ILS language. The task of running the SPV is relatively easy—except when it is not. The manager, as with all agents, must be sufficiently alert to unusual circumstances to be able to adjust intelligently to the letter of his mandate. Similarly, the trust must be one that protects both the issuer and investor alike. Issuers will want to be assured that the money to compensate them for loss is available when needed. This means making sure that it is invested in only the most secure collateral. They should also want a structure that is cancelable if, for whatever reason, the value of their protection diminishes. Investors also want their investment to be returned if the ILS runs loss-free and is protected against improper collection by the cedant.

Structure of the Bond

Another raft of decisions concerns the structure of the bond itself. Should the issue be a one-off transaction, or should it be part of a regular program? Each will have an impact on documentation. Should the term of the bond be one year or multiple years? Should the bond risk be resettable or coupon-adjusted? There are many such structural decisions that the banker, the risk modeler, and the cedant will need to decide on. And when all are put together they will have to be enshrined in a legal private placement memorandum. Thus the legal firm is also a most important choice.

The Law Firm

The sponsor, in conjunction with the investment bankers, will select attorneys to represent its interests and draft the transaction documents. It will also need a law firm in the jurisdiction of the chosen SPV to contend with local issues. These firms should be experienced in insurance law as well as securities law. There are a number of firms in New York and Chicago (such as Cadwalader, Wickersham & Taft LLP, or Sidley Austin LLP), as well as in the most common SPV jurisdictions—Bermuda, Cayman Islands, and Dublin.

Case Study

United Services Automobile Association (USAA)
- First issuance: 1996
- Original issue size: US$500 million
- Original issue structure: double trigger with indemnity and index contingents
- Subsequent issues: all indemnity
- Initial coverage: coastal wind
- Subsequent coverage: all US Wind and Quake
- Most tranches occurrence-based, some aggregate
- Maturity of typical structure: 3 years
- Typical number of tranches annually: 4
- Number of years of consecutive issuance: 16

- Total issuance to date: US$4.8 billion
- Smallest issuance year: US$125 million
- Largest issuance year: US$700 million
- Currently outstanding: approximately US$1.3 billion

Conclusion

Compare the Alternatives

Best practice requires that the cedant compare and contrast the ILS alternative with more traditional protection possibilities. This goes beyond just checking for one deal; it means doing the comparison on a regular and consistent basis. This ensures that the best deal is acquired for shareholders or policyholders. There is one firm that has set the gold standard in this regard—USAA. It has issued for 16 years in a row. It has always issued indemnity cover, after building trust in its first few years with an event cover. And it has always simultaneously bought protection in both the traditional market and the ILS market. Finally, it has displayed great adaptability in its coverage, responding to its own needs, presumably with the trust of its investors.

Reiterate

No securitization forms perfectly the instant after an initial decision to proceed has been made. It requires going back over the analysis and double checking the assumptions, prices, etc., to see if it still meets objectives before moving to the "execute" decision. The last step in the process must therefore be the step of rechecking and reiterating through the procedures.

As the market grows and reissues take place, the practice elements listed here become more routine. Persistent issuers such as USAA will follow a regular procedural calendar over several months. They know where they are going and the touch points that must be visited. They know the speed at which they are comfortable putting the components together. First-time issuers will likely need to spend a period of up to six months to go through a thorough process, but depending on the simplicity of the structure, the whole process can be accomplished in as little as 10–12 weeks. If we think of protection buying as raising surrogate capital, these times and procedures compare favorably with other markets that raise debt, equity, or indeed traditional reinsurance protection.

More Info

Books:

Lane, Morton (ed). *Alternative Risk Strategies*. London: Risk Books, 2003.

Kunreuther, Howard C., and Erwann O. Michel-Kerjan, with Neil A. Doherty *et al*. *At War With the Weather: Managing Large-Scale Risks in a New Era of Catastrophes*. Cambridge, MA: MIT Press, 2009.

Himick, Michael (ed). *Securitized Insurance Risk, Strategic Opportunities for Insurers and Investors*. Chicago, IL: Glenlake Publishing, 1998.

Culp, Christopher L. *Structured Finance and Insurance: The ART of Managing Capital and Risk*. Hoboken, NJ: Wiley, 2006.

Froot, Kenneth A. (ed). *The Financing of Catastrophe Risk*. Chicago, IL: University of Chicago Press, 1999.

Tang, Kenny (ed). *Weather Risk Management: A Guide for Corporations, Hedge Funds and Investors*. London: Risk Books, 2010.

Websites:

Artemis: www.artemis.bm

Aon Benfield Securities: www.aon.com/reinsurance

Global Reinsurance: www.globalreinsurance.com

Guy Carpenter & Company: www.guycarp.com/portal/extranet/insights/insights.html?vid=5

Insurance Insider: www.insuranceinsider.com

Lane Financial: www.lanefinancialllc.com

Reactions: www.reactionsnet.com

Swiss Re Sigma: www.swissre.com/sigma

Trading Risk: www.trading-risk.com

Obstacles to the Further Development of the Longevity Swaps Market for Pension Funds

by Martin Bird and Tim Gordon

This Chapter Covers

- Why the United Kingdom is currently the most fertile locale for longevity swaps.
- Why longevity risk protection can appear expensive to pension funds.
- Why index-based longevity solutions are currently uncompetitive compared with bespoke longevity swaps and are likely to remain so for the foreseeable future.
- Why lack of standardization remains a key obstacle to the wider use of longevity swaps.
- Drivers pushing the continued expansion of the UK longevity swaps market.

Introduction

The combined liabilities of occupational pension plans in the United Kingdom are around £1 trillion. These liabilities are predominantly defined-benefit, consisting of immediate and deferred annuities, and therefore the majority of the benefit payments depend on the longevity of the beneficiaries. Given that these pension plans are materially exposed to longevity risk—i.e. the risk that their beneficiaries may live longer than expected—and the trend over the past decade has been to reduce asset–liability mismatching, it is reasonable to ask why UK pension plans have not done more to mitigate their longevity risk. There are, very broadly, only two means of removing longevity risk in a defined-benefit pension plan:

- secure the liabilities completely with an insurance company (which may or may not involve the plan winding up);

- take out a longevity swap with an insurance company or investment bank, i.e. receive cash flows that no longer depend on the longevity of the beneficiaries in return for the plan's longevity-dependent cash flows plus a fee.

The question we address in this chapter is why longevity swap transactions are currently running at around only £3 billion to £5 billion per year in the context of total liabilities of around £1 trillion.

We should probably start by noting that in the United Kingdom a number of factors combine to explain why it is the most fertile locale for longevity swaps.

- *There is a large company-sponsored defined-benefit occupational pensions sector.*

- *Pension plans are funded.* Having to put real cash into pension plans focuses the mind remarkably compared with adding numbers to a balance sheet on what is typically an unrealistic basis. The UK regulatory regime also requires that pension plan assets are held in trust, meaning that pension plan funding is treated very seriously.

- *Companies bear the deficit risk.* In many other countries, companies with large defined-benefit pension plan deficits can walk away from them, but in the United Kingdom this is not possible.

- *Index-linked pension increases.* Quite simply, pension increases make longer-dated cash flows more valuable, and it is for these cash flows that longevity risk really bites. The legacy of high inflation in the 1970s has resulted in the United Kingdom having some of the strongest statutory inflation-proofing of pensions in payment and in deferment. By way of contrast, pension increases are almost unheard of in US pension plans.

Other countries that are prime candidates for future use of longevity swaps are Canada, the United States, and the Netherlands—with Canada being favorite. In the United States, pension increases ("cost of living allowances") are uncommon and the law has been changed recently to allow members to surrender pensions in exchange for payment of a lump sum. This probably explains why the big US longevity deals, for example GM's group annuity purchase in 2012, have been bulk annuities rather than pure longevity swaps—i.e. they are not primarily about longevity risk. In the Netherlands, it is not clear at the time of writing that pension plans fully bear longevity risk, so that market is in something of a state of flux.

It therefore seems sensible to focus on the UK market given that it is currently the trailblazer for longevity swaps. It is no coincidence that the UK actuarial profession has developed a sophisticated two-dimensional (i.e. depending on age and birth year) mortality projections model that is updated every year, while actuaries in many other countries are using one-dimensional (i.e. dependent only on age) projections that are sometimes a decade or more out of date. The reason is simple: in the UK the financial impact of longevity is material and therefore it is vital to get this right.

But—and it is a big but—it remains true that pension plan funding is treated very differently to insurance company reserving. Occupational pension plans started out providing what were essentially discretionary benefits and, despite the huge amount of legislation creep that has turned them into promises and foisted unforeseen levels of liability on companies, the regulation and culture of pension funding still reflects their origin. A defined-benefit pension plan in the United Kingdom, United States, or Canada is typically funded without risk reserves, or, if risk reserves are allowed for, they are typically much lower than the statutory reserves that insurance companies are required to hold. The notion that things will "work out in the long term" has been remarkably persistent in the pensions world, even though at the same time the insurance world in Europe has been ramping up its risk reserving requirements with the imminent introduction of Solvency II. It is still common practice for pension plans to invest in risky assets without corresponding risk reserves (other than an implicit reliance on sponsor covenant). In contrast, insurance companies are required to hold higher reserves the more mismatched the investment strategy is relative to the liabilities.

Until it becomes standard to maintain reserves explicitly for longevity risk in the pensions world, it will remain a struggle even to get longevity risk solutions on the agenda for many pension plans. And until pensions legislation changes, longevity swaps are likely to continue to appear expensive for nonpensioners.

Longevity Index Solutions

An obvious solution is to provide a standard medium of exchange for longevity risk. This has received a lot of attention, initially being developed by JP Morgan through the LifeMetrics framework and then more recently through the Life & Longevity Markets Association (LLMA) based in London, whose stated aim is "to promote a liquid traded market in longevity and mortality-related risk." The idea is that longevity indices can form the basis for a traded market in longevity risk which would, in turn, facilitate access to longevity risk protection and price discovery. This is a laudable objective, but the generic longevity index approach currently seems to be stalled.

In order to be suitable, a longevity index needs to be based on mortality experience data with strong assurances concerning:

- stability of the definition of the population on which it is based;
- sufficient past data to measure risk;
- the availability of future data, along with their objectivity and reliability.

For UK pension schemes, the only population that meets these criteria is the national mortality data set as measured by the Office for National Statistics (ONS). However, the recent restatement[1] of England and Wales mortality experience data (specifically, the population data) has illustrated that even nationally produced longevity indices are not 100% reliable.

The main problem is that longevity risk is not fungible—i.e. the future improvements in longevity for one group of individuals will not be the same as for another—and therefore one cannot reliably offset the longevity risk for one sector of the population against the longevity risk for a different one. This gives rise to basis risk, i.e. the risk that the mortality experience of the wider population on which the index is based will differ from the population at risk. Pension plan populations in particular differ from the national population because their members tend to be better off and, in addition, the liability impact is weighted toward the even better-off.

Even quantifying longevity basis risk is difficult. Not only do we not have good-quality data on past mortality experience by subpopulation, but even if we did we would still struggle. This is because it is almost impossible to determine whether a past difference between longevity improvements for different populations will:

- continue into the future, i.e. the longevity of the different populations will continue to diverge forever;

- fall to zero, i.e. the difference between the different populations will remain at its current level; or

- reverse, i.e. the longevities of the different populations will reconverge.

We can find examples of each of the above by comparing different national mortality data sets. In particular, the difference between male and female mortality rates provides a striking example of mortality reconvergence in the United Kingdom and other Western World countries. If, in 1970, one had assumed that past differences between male and female longevity improvement would persist, the assumption would have led to a massive understatement of male longevity improvement. So basis risk is not only difficult to quantify, but given the wider possible range of outcomes it seems that it is necessarily quite large. And given that index solutions rely on leveraging to be effective, the basis risk is magnified still further.

There are other problems.

- Although longevity index forwards are sometimes portrayed as being analogous to forwards in other markets, longevity has more dimensions because it is age-dependent. They are not simple to work with and introduce an additional step into the hedging process—i.e. the need to determine an optimal combination of various forward contracts, which is an ongoing process. By way of contrast, under a normal longevity swap structure, there is no need to calibrate, reconcile risk, and/or rebalance over time.

- q- and S-forwards, the index contracts that have been suggested to date (LLMA, 2010), are zero-coupon structures and therefore are likely to be more expensive than a normal longevity swap. The underlying exits, i.e. capital markets and reinsurers, typically prefer a payout profile that pays an income. An investment bank therefore has to transform the forward starting q/S-forward structure into a coupon-paying structure for the exits. It would be cleaner (for example, there would be no queries or additional credit charges from the bank's internal credit management) if the bank could simply pass on the swap cash flows without such manipulation.

- q- and S-forwards are written in nominal sterling, whereas UK pension plan cash flows tend to be linked to inflation, requiring a further layer of intermediation.

What all this means is that, at present, using longevity index solutions is materially more expensive than a bespoke longevity swap, while at the same incurring a material but difficult-to-quantity basis risk. It should therefore come as no surprise that, at the time of writing, activity in index-based longevity swaps is somewhere between nil and small compared with bespoke swaps. It would be a hugely positive development if we had a large and liquid longevity index market, but we expect that the future will instead see quirky, one-off index-based trades.

Expanding the Existing Longevity Swap Model

Having ruled out longevity index solutions as likely in the future, we are left with existing bespoke longevity swaps, i.e. swaps on the specific individuals in the population at risk. In the United Kingdom this market has grown from a standing start in 2009 to around £3 billion to £5 billion a year in 2011 and 2012. To put this in context, over the period 2000–12, UK plan sponsors settled liabilities in the bulk annuity market (buy-ins and buy-outs) to the tune of around £30 billion, whereas more than £19 billion of longevity liabilities have been hedged over the past three years. We think that this growth in longevity swaps is impressive and a testimony to the determination of pension plan trustees and sponsoring companies to address risk management seriously.

Table 1 provides details of the major longevity swaps to date. It is immediately obvious that the majority of these deals are large, typically over £1 billion—implying that at the moment the fixed element of implementation and monitoring costs makes longevity swaps financially viable only for large pension plans.

Table 1. UK pension fund longevity swap trades to date

Date	Fund	Provider	Liabilities hedged[1] (£ million)	Deal type[2]
March 2013	Bentley Motors	Abbey Life, Deutsche Bank	400	Bespoke swap
February 2013	BAE	L&G	3,200	Bespoke swap
December 2012	LV=	Swiss Re	800	Bespoke swap (including nonpensioners)
May 2012	AkzoNobel	Swiss Re	1,400	Bespoke swap
January 2012	Pilkington	Legal & General	1,100	Bespoke swap
December 2011	British Airways	Goldman Sachs, Rothesay Life	1,300	Bespoke swap
November 2011	Rolls-Royce	Deutsche Bank	3,000	Bespoke swap
August 2011	ITV	Credit Suisse	1,700	Bespoke swap
February 2011	Pall UK Pension Fund	JP Morgan	70	Nonpensioner index-based hedge
July 2010	British Airways	Goldman Sachs, Rothesay Life	1,300	Bespoke synthetic buy-in
February 2010	BMW	Abbey Life, Deutsche Bank	3,000	Bespoke swap
November 2009	Royal County of Berkshire Pension Fund	Swiss Re	1,000	Bespoke swap
July 2009	RSA Insurance Group	Goldman Sachs, Rothesay Life	1,900	Bespoke synthetic buy-in
May 2009	Babcock	Credit Suisse	1,500	Bespoke swap

1. Approximate figure based on publicly available information.
2. Solely pensioner-related unless otherwise specified.
Source: Aon Hewitt.

This is partly because the regulatory regime in the United Kingdom has resulted in pension plan benefit structures that are notoriously complex. Further, pension plan trustees are often reluctant to simplify reinsured risks because that entails retaining remote residual risks. This is not unreasonable—compared with professional investors with a portfolio of assets or liabilities, trustees are responsible for their pension plan in isolation, i.e. they do not have a portfolio of pension plans over which to diversify risk. Finally, pension plans need to have one eye on their ultimate exit strategy. Awkward residual differences between actual pension plan liabilities and those covered by the longevity swap may be expensive or impossible to buy out on eventual wind-up. This is less of an issue for very large pension plans, which realistically do not expect to wind up for the next 20 years, but it is a genuine concern for medium to large pension plans.

Possibly the greatest obstacle is lack of standardization. Longevity swaps are still relatively new, and each deal results in some form of innovation. And there is a bewildering array of options to choose from—for example, whether the contract is insurance- or derivative-based, the degree of precise replication of benefit indexation, the terms for exit options, whether collateral is provided via security interest or title transfer, and so on. So we are left in a chicken and egg situation. Very large pension schemes can afford to do things differently and therefore they do so, but the next rung down needs more standardization before longevity swaps can become cost-effective. Think Betamax vs VHS (or HD DVD vs Blu-ray)—once a standard was settled on, the market exploded. And the more standardized longevity swaps become, the more likely insurers are to treat them as plan assets and incorporate them as part of the purchase price at fair value if a pension plan winds up, removing one of the current obstacles to adoption. We think that progress is being made, but it will take a few years yet for the longevity swap to become a universal model.

In the meantime, there are plenty of drivers pushing the expansion of the longevity swaps market.

- Awareness of longevity risk continues to increase. The large group annuity deals in the United States have raised awareness globally.

- Although it might appear that the reduced number of intermediaries in the UK market is a negative, the reality is the opposite. Pricing is actually determined by the reinsurance market and the number of longevity reinsurers has increased, as have their capacity limits as they have become more comfortable with longevity risk as an insurance class.

- Pension plans continue to mature, i.e. to have relatively more pensioner-to-nonpensioner liability. Longevity swap pricing tends to be more attractive to pension plans for pensioners.

- The continued underfunding of pension plans makes longevity swaps relatively more attractive to pension plans compared with bulk annuities because it allows them to retain control over their assets, for example for outperformance.

- There has been repeated interest from capital market investors, which suggests that there is additional capacity waiting to be tapped. Standardization would be particularly helpful in this context.

Conclusions

We expect that the UK longevity swaps market will continue to grow as pension plans continue to bear down on risk generally and continue to mature. In most other defined benefit-oriented countries, the regulatory regime and/or no pension increases mean that pension plan longevity risk is typically not as financially material as in the United Kingdom. We therefore do not expect to see longevity swaps make as much inroad in these countries, although we do consider it reasonably likely that a major non-UK pension plan will implement a longevity swap within the next couple of years.

Index-based longevity solutions have failed to take off so far. Moreover, the problems associated with them, most notably basis risk, mean that we are skeptical about their future as a vehicle for pension plans to mitigate their longevity risk. Index-based solutions may, however, have a role to play as a means of exchanging longevity risk between insurers.

Finally, we expect implementation costs to reduce over time as longevity swap contracts gradually become more standardized.

More Info

Report:
Life & Longevity Markets Association. "Longevity pricing framework: A framework for pricing longevity exposures developed by the LLMA." October 29, 2010. Online at: tinyurl.com/ln29zgn [PDF].

Websites:
Continuous Mortality Investigation: tinyurl.com/ll7gzhc

Life & Longevity Markets Association (LLMA): www.llma.org

Office for National Statistics (ONS; UK): www.ons.gov.uk

1 Office for National Statistics. "Statistical bulletin: Population estimates for England and Wales, mid-2002 to mid-2010 revised (National)." December 13, 2012. Online at: www.ons.gov.uk/ons/dcp171778_288817.pdf

Longevity and Annuities— The Challenge of Giving a Secure Pension

by Dominic Grimley

This Chapter Covers

In recent years, the cost of securing a pension has been very volatile. At the same time, the demand for annuities has continued to increase significantly, with more currently latent demand expected to surface once more company pension schemes can afford to buy annuities in bulk. This raises questions about the capacity in the annuity market and the drivers for pricing, as considered in this article. Topics covered are:

- The difficulty of estimating longevity accurately.
- The impact of longevity and other factors on annuities.
- The stresses and strains in the annuities market focusing on the United Kingdom.

Introduction

Life expectancy has improved substantially in the United Kingdom; we know this because the country has a relatively strong record of storing and analyzing data on deaths. Annuity providers have models to consider how life expectancy varies by age, gender, and wealth; and how benefit size and postcode can indicate the likely wealth of people. Where health and lifestyle information is available, the calculation can be refined much further to take into account the likely impact of this information. To consider likely future trends, these firms monitor the latest research on the underlying causes of death—with the big killers being heart attacks, strokes, and cancers—and on new healthcare improvements.

However, this does not lead to a clear answer for future changes in life expectancy. Healthcare innovations may reduce a cause of death, but may increase the incidence of other alternative ailments in later life. What we can say with certainty is that the current rate of increase in life expectancy is beyond what the originators of annuity policies considered 20 or even 10 years ago.

Over time, when we compare the life expectancy improvements which have been anticipated with those that have actually transpired over the years, there has been consistent underestimation of how much longer we will live in the future. So although research into this area has increased dramatically in recent years, giving much more knowledge about the key questions affecting longevity, it is less clear whether this has given narrower answers for future experience.

Longer lives may be good news for us on the face of it, but they are a major issue for providing a pension promise, since the cost and uncertainty over funding the promise are substantially increased.

From the standpoint of employers, longevity risks are one of many factors that have encouraged the closure of most final-salary pension schemes in the private sector. Closure stops further pension being built up, but still leaves the uncertainty over the cost of the benefits already earned, which can only be fully addressed by purchasing annuities to pass these pension commitments to an insurance company.

The government, too, would love to be able to move away from guaranteeing a set level of benefit but, so far, it has only proved possible to restrain rather than stop the continued granting of pension promises in the public sector.

Impacts on Annuity Pricing

To say that annuity prices have been rising in recent years would be something of an understatement. Annuity prices have been driven upwards by a series of factors coming together:

- The main asset class used for pricing annuities is bonds, and bond yields have fallen substantially, particularly since the summer of 2011. This means that insurers need to pay more for bonds to cover the same volume of annuity business—and that increases the price of annuities and worsens the annuity rate offered.

- The fall in yields has been exacerbated by government initiatives to kickstart their economies through quantitative easing programs. These were implemented by the central banks buying back bonds, which drives up bond prices and further reduces the yield on bonds.

- The expectations for inflation did not fall with the fall in yields. This has made the cost of a pension with inflation protection (a common feature of UK schemes) look particularly expensive.

- Regulation has been tightening for insurance companies, as mentioned further below, pushing upwards the reserves required to back an annuity.

In this environment, increases in life expectancy have not been as visible in their impact on annuities. But annuities are sensitive to life expectancy—a one-year increase in life expectancy can increase an annuity by as much as 4%. So, improved life expectancy has steadily pushed up annuity prices, while the low-yield environment has produced more of a sudden and perhaps reversible shift in recent years.

In December 2012, one more factor pushed up prices in Europe. From that point—for some—annuity prices could not take into account the differences in life expectancy for males and females. This unisex pricing requirement has so far only taken effect in the individual annuity market, and so has not made pricing any worse for company schemes buying "bulk" annuities.

Uncertain Regulation

Since the credit crunch, the monitoring regimes for financial institutions have been under scrutiny. In the United Kingdom, the responsibilities of the Financial Services Authority (which regulated a range of financial institutions) have been split. A new regulator, the Prudential Regulation Authority, took responsibility for annuity providers in April 2013.

The key UK and EU regulations in place remain the same for now, although there has been pressure applied to providers since the credit crunch, to justify their investment strategies and the allowance in their reserves for future asset defaults in different economic scenarios. Some insurers have significantly increased their asset default allowances since 2008 as a result.

New EU regulations (Solvency II) are still awaited after some years of gestation, through there remains substantial uncertainty over how they will be implemented. An extreme interpretation of Solvency II could push insurers to hold risk-free assets against their annuity book. Since the returns on risk-free assets are very low, this again would drive up the price of annuities substantially.

There is an interesting conundrum in all of this for governments as they think about ways of getting individuals to take greater responsibility for their own pensions rather than relying on the state or, given the closure of final-salary schemes, their employer. If the life insurance industry is forced to play too safe and so price annuities more conservatively, people will be reluctant to build up funds to buy annuities. With current low yields, the return on annuities is barely enough to cover expected inflation.

From a UK perspective, the recent launch of auto-enrolment is putting considerably more people into money purchase schemes, from which most would ultimately buy an annuity, so an improvement in annuity rates would be very welcome.

UK Annuity Market Capacity

Estimates vary, but the pension promises in defined-benefit schemes across the private sector may amount to as much as £2 trillion. In contrast, the amount of these promises secured in the annuity market has typically been around £5 billion per year—which means that, once allowance is made for the limited number of schemes still allowing benefits to be earned, the total amount of unsecured pension is unlikely to have even started to fall yet. So, if there is an overall expectation of the buyout of these many schemes through annuities, this project is very much still in its infancy.

Clearly there will be a growing desire for employers to de-risk and de-commission closed schemes, as they increasingly relate to legacy pension promises. Many employers have considered securing bulk annuities but have typically not proceeded since the credit crunch, as adverse market conditions have left the available scheme assets some way short of annuity costs. This has left substantial latent demand for later bulk annuity purchases.

A positive signal, such as a partial move away from the low-yield environment seen over 2011–13, could give a substantial but unpredictable growth in annuity tenders from company schemes.

In turn, the individual annuity market continues to grow, as more people reach retirement with benefits partly earned in a money purchase scheme. This market has so far typically been around £12bn in size in recent years, but should steadily become much bigger.

This raises questions over annuity market capacity.

In terms of assets, a key investment class for most UK annuity providers is corporate debt. The UK corporate debt market is around £500 billion in size, with only part of its stocks likely to offer the right characteristics in terms of quality, term, and diversification to satisfy annuity providers—and with other investors of course making use of this market as well. There is clearly a limit to how far this can be used to match UK pension risks. Hence, the annuity providers are looking more widely than ever to find alternative assets which, if held, would offer an acceptable balance of quality, liability matching, return, and justifiable reserving requirements. This last point is a key consideration, as more unstable assets come with substantial implications for the additional contingency reserves an insurance company must hold against a possible fall in their value.

Ultimately, a more crucial question for capacity may be who wants to end up with the longevity risk. At present, some annuity providers are happy to bear much of the longevity risk that they have taken on, while others pass most of it on to the reinsurance market. The longevity reinsurance market currently has substantial capacity and a wide range of participants. It is a global market, and there are other countries where this longevity capacity is being used, notably the United States recently. The longevity reinsurance capacity is finite and ultimately likely to be tested, with new market participants becoming needed to take on some of the longevity risk, perhaps in smaller securitized and standardized chunks of risk. There have been moves to create this wider longevity market, but so far it remains an aspiration. At some point it may become essential.

Conclusion

For companies looking to secure their schemes' pension promises, and for individuals looking to buy an annuity at retirement, an understanding of the factors affecting annuity pricing, and advance preparation and monitoring, are likely to be key factors for reaching an annuity purchase without a shock.

A key question is when to de-risk the assets held ahead of an annuity purchase—higher annuity costs may mean that more asset returns are needed to build up a big enough fund. But while the pension assets are being selected for growth, they are unlikely to also provide a stable relationship with annuity prices, leaving the funding position volatile until the assets are moved towards long-dated bond stocks. With both high returns and low downside risk not easily available together, the typical solution will also involve spending more money on funding pensions than was previously planned.

The annuity markets remain competitive, and available terms will vary as market conditions change. This gives a definite advantage for a buyer who knows in advance the annuity product they are looking for, and has prepared as far as possible to be able to transact when the sums start to add up.

But being prepared could become a more critical factor than this, for companies looking to secure sizeable bulk annuity deals. As the same changes in market conditions may create trigger points for annuity transactions for a wide range of schemes, annuity provider capacity— both financial capacity and also manpower capacity—may suddenly be tested. The nimblest and most prepared schemes may then be preferred, as the easiest route to new business being secured by a then more selective annuity provider.

Should Governments Step In and Start Issuing Longevity Bonds?[1]

by David Blake, Tom Boardman, and Andrew Cairns

This Chapter Covers

- Systematic longevity risk is a risk that cannot be hedged with existing financial instruments.

- Governments could help pension plans and annuity providers to hedge systematic longevity risk by issuing longevity bonds in exchange for receiving a longevity risk premium.

- This would enable the private sector to deliver more secure pensions and better-valued annuities.

- There is growing international support for governments to issue longevity bonds from bodies such as the Organisation for Economic Co-operation and Development (OECD), World Economic Forum and International Monetary Fund (IMF).

Overview

Insurance companies and defined-benefit plans face the risk that retirees might live longer than expected. This risk might adversely affect both the willingness and ability of financial institutions to supply retired households with financial products to manage their wealth decumulation (the conversion of a person's accumulated pension assets into pension income). Longevity bonds are instruments that would allow financial institutions to hedge systematic (or aggregate) longevity risk. These bonds, which involve no repayment of principal, would pay a coupon that is linked to the survivorship of a cohort, say 65-year-old males born in 1945. The coupon rate in any year would reflect the actual survivorship of this cohort. If a higher than expected proportion of this cohort survived to, say, age 80—a development that would cost the insurance company or pension plan more than expected—the coupon rate would increase, allowing the providers to offset some of their cost. Alternatively, if a lower proportion of the cohort survived, then the coupon would be reduced. The key questions of interest are how longevity bonds would work in practice, who could issue them, and how would they be priced.

This chapter highlights the benefits that could flow from a transparent and liquid capital market in longevity-linked instruments, and argues that the government could play an important role in helping this market to grow. The line of reasoning comes from the United Kingdom, but it has validity for all countries with mature funded pension systems.

Why Worry about Longevity Risk?

Longevity risk is borne by every institution making payments that depend on how long individuals are going to live. These include sponsors of defined-benefit pension plans in the private sector, insurance companies selling life annuities, and governments through the social security system and the defined-benefit plans they sponsor for public-sector employees.

Longevity risk consists of random variation risk and trend risk (Figure 1). Random variation risk exists because some people will die before their life expectancy and some will die after. Trend risk involves the possibility that unanticipated changes in lifestyle or medical advances significantly improve the average longevity of all the members of a particular birth cohort.[2]

Figure 1. Decomposition of longevity risk

Total longevity risk

=

Systematic longevity risk
(Trend risk)

Government needs to provide hedge

+

Specific longevity risk
(Random variation risk)

Private sector can hedge

Private-sector institutions can reduce random variation risk by pooling and relying on the law of large numbers to reduce the degree of variability as the size of the pool increases. Trend risk, on the other hand, is a "systematic risk" that cannot be diversified away by pooling. The private sector is unable to hedge this risk effectively without a suitable hedging instrument.

The presence of such a nonhedgeable risk in the face of an increasing demand for annuities creates two problems. First, a big growth in annuities could result in an unhealthy concentration of risk among a small number of insurance companies, leading to possible insolvency should mortality rates decline faster than forecast. Second, the capital in the insurance/reinsurance industry is insufficient to deal with total global private-sector longevity risk. European Union regulators have proposed that additional capital should be required for liabilities with nonhedgeable risks.[3] The cost of the extra capital would have to be passed on to customers, resulting in a reduction of up to 10% in the income annuities can provide. Longevity bonds address both these problems.

How Can Longevity Bonds Hedge Systematic Longevity Risk?

To see how a longevity bond can hedge systematic longevity risk requires both a quantification of longevity risk and identifying where it is concentrated. Figure 2 presents a survivor fan chart, which shows the uncertainty surrounding projections of the number of survivors to each age from the cohort of males from England and Wales who were aged 65 at the end of 2006.[4] The shaded areas in each bar are the 90% confidence interval, and the line in the middle of each shaded area indicates the proportion of the cohort expected to survive to each age. Uncertainty is low at younger ages; one can be fairly confident that about 80% of 65-year-olds will survive to 75. Uncertainty increases thereafter and peaks at age 93. The best estimate is that 36% will survive to age 90, but it could be anywhere between 30% and 41%, a very large range. Figure 2 also shows the so-called "tail risk"—that is, the probability that some members of this cohort will live well beyond 100.

Figure 2. Survivor fan chart for males aged 65. (Derived from the Cairns, Blake, and Dowd (2006) stochastic mortality model estimated on English and Welsh male mortality data for 65-year-olds over the period 1991–2006.)

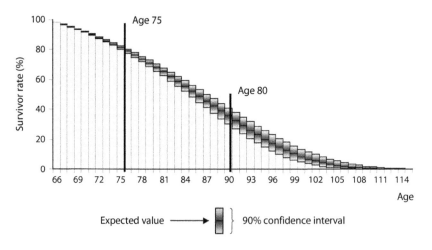

Consider how a longevity bond with the following characteristics can help to hedge systematic longevity risk:

- the bond coupons payable each year will depend on the proportion of a given cohort that is alive in that year—for example, the percentage of men born in 1945, and who were age 65 in 2010, that survives to 2011, 2012, and so on;

- coupon payments are not made for ages for which longevity risk is low—for example, the first coupon might not be paid until the cohort reaches age 75 (such a bond would be called a deferred longevity bond);

- the coupon payments continue until the maturity date of the bond, which might, for example, be 40 years after the issue date when the cohort of males reaches age 105;

- the bond pays coupons only and has no repayment of principal.[5]

Figure 3. Deferred longevity bond for male aged 65 with 10-year deferment. The longevity bond is payable from age 75 with a terminal payment at age 105 to cover post-105 longevity risk. (Chart derived as noted for Figure 2.)

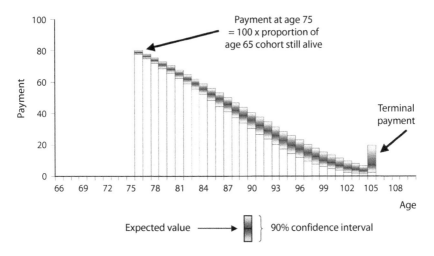

Figure 3 shows the possible range of coupon payments on such a deferred longevity bond based on the population of English and Welsh males aged 65 at the end of 2006. If population survivorship is higher at each age than expected, the bond pays out higher coupons. This pattern helps pension plans and annuity providers to meet the higher-than-expected pension and annuity payments which they need to make. If, on the other hand, survivorship is lower at each age than expected, the bond pays out lower coupons. But the pension plans and annuity providers are not likely to mind, since their pension and annuity payments are also likely to be lower.

The bond will provide a *perfect* hedge only for pension plans and annuity providers with plan members/annuitants who have exactly the same mortality experience over time as the cohort underlying the bond. If the plan members/annuitants have a mortality experience that differs from that of the national population, it will introduce basis risk. In practice, some basis risk will remain.[6]

In theory, longevity bonds could be issued for both males and females, for each age, and for each socioeconomic group. Such granularity of the longevity bond market would allow a high degree of hedge effectiveness to be achieved. But it would also result in negligible liquidity or pricing transparency: the more bonds there are, the less trading in each bond and the less frequently the bonds will be priced in the market. As with other markets—especially derivatives markets—a small number of suitably designed bonds should provide an appropriate balance between hedge effectiveness, liquidity, and pricing transparency (Blake, Cairns, and Dowd, 2006).

Who Could Issue Longevity Bonds?

In principle, longevity bonds could be issued by private-sector organizations. Some argue that pharmaceutical companies would be natural issuers, since the longer people live, the more they will spend on medicines (Dowd, 2003). While the theory may be correct, the scale of the demand for longevity bonds far exceeds the conceivable supply from such companies. Further, significant credit risk would be associated with the private-sector issuance of an instrument that is intended to hedge a systematic risk for many years into the future.

A more realistic issuer of longevity bonds would be the government.[7] The government may be better able to issue longevity bonds in the required volume, and it also has an interest in promoting an efficient and well-functioning annuity market, safeguarding the solvency of insurance companies and facilitating the efficient spreading of longevity risk via the development of a capital market in longevity risk transfers.[8]

Although the government would play a key role in getting the market started, eventually its role could be limited to providing tail risk protection. That is, once the market for longevity bonds has matured, in the sense of producing stable and reliable price points in the age range 65–90 along the longevity risk term structure[9] (Figure 4), the capital markets could take over responsibility for providing the necessary hedging capacity in this age range. All that might then be needed would be for the government to provide a continuous supply of deferred tail longevity bonds with payments starting at, say, age 90.[10]

Figure 5 illustrates the cash flows on such a bond. These bonds will allow for hedging of longevity risk and allow investors who have recently become interested in taking the other side of the longevity swaps market to avoid assuming long-duration tail longevity risk, a risk for which they have no appetite.

Figure 4. Longevity bond cash flows across ages and time

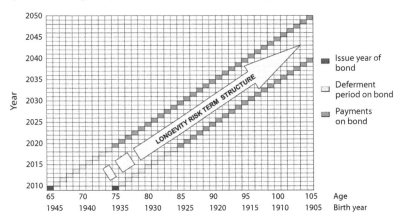

Figure 5. Deferred tail longevity bond for male aged 65. The longevity bond is payable from age 90 with a terminal payment at age 105 to cover post-105 longevity risk. (Chart derived as noted for Figure 2.)

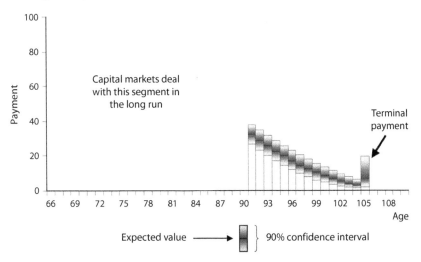

Some contend that the government is not a natural issuer of longevity bonds because of its large existing exposure to longevity risk through the social security system and pensions for public employees. Here several considerations may be relevant. First, the government would receive a longevity risk premium from issuing the bonds—that is, the issuance would generate revenue above the expected cost of paying the bond's coupons. Second, the government could offset the cost of paying higher than expected coupons—as a result of the population living longer—by increasing the state pension age.[11] Third, the issuance of longevity bonds should result in a more efficient annuity market and hence higher incomes in retirement, perhaps reducing the need for means-tested retirement benefits. Fourth, the benefits to government finances would start to accrue immediately, whereas the tail risk protection provided by deferred tail longevity bonds would only start to be payable 25 years in the future when the first insured cohort turned 90. Finally, one could argue that issuing longevity bonds is consistent with the government's role of facilitating intergenerational risk sharing: only the government can legally enforce intergenerational contracts.

The quantity of bonds issued will depend, in part, on price, and this will be considered in the next section. However, the total issuance is likely to be small in relation to the overall size of the government bond market.

Pricing Considerations

Ultimately, the demand for longevity bonds will depend on their price. The government will likely be able to charge a risk premium—i.e., the price at which the government will be able to sell the bond will exceed the expected present value of the coupons payable on the bond, discounted by the interest rate on government securities of comparable maturities. The reason is that insurance companies holding longevity bonds will need to hold less capital against the risk of mortality improvements (people living longer) being more rapid than expected. But it is unlikely that the desired market for longevity bonds will develop if the government just focuses on insurers. The bonds will need to be priced to also attract sponsors of defined-benefit plans, which do not currently face solvency capital requirements. Other investors, including investment banks, will also be discouraged from buying longevity bonds if they believe that the longevity risk premium is excessive, because they will fear that the bonds will eventually fall in value.

Summary and Further Steps

Many parties would gain from having a market price for longevity risk and the ability to hedge systematic longevity risk. The expected cost of government borrowing will decline because investors seeking protection against longevity risk will be willing to accept a lower return than on comparable government securities. The government, as regulator, would also benefit. A longevity risk term structure should help the regulators to calculate any risk-based levy to government-operated pension insurance funds, such as those administered by the US Pension Benefit Guaranty Corporation and the UK Pension Protection Fund.

In the private sector, sponsors of defined-benefit plans would have the opportunity to reduce longevity risks. Insurers could quantify the market value of their longevity risk exposure. The ability to hedge longevity risk would reduce insurers' capital requirements, which is a potentially important consideration should the demand for annuities increase. Longevity bonds would also reduce the concentration of longevity risk among insurers by facilitating the spread of longevity risk around the capital markets. And investors would gain access to a new asset class whose returns are uncorrelated with traditional asset classes, such as bonds, equities, and real estate.

The introduction of government-issued longevity bonds is a clear win-win situation for the private and public sectors alike.

As a next step, it is recommended that a government considering the introduction of such bonds establish a working party to:

- undertake a cost–benefit analysis of the government's issuance of longevity bonds;

- determine the scale of longevity risk that it would be assuming;

- consider actions the government could take to mitigate this risk;

- work through the practicalities of government issuance of longevity bonds, including issues such as: the reference mortality indices for determining coupon payments; potential demand; pricing; liquidity and tax.

Appendix: Support for Government Issuance of Longevity Bonds

The following organizations have shown support for government-issued longevity bonds.

UK Pensions Commission

The Pensions Commission in the United Kingdom suggested that the government should consider the use of longevity bonds to absorb tail risk for those aged over 90 or 95 *provided that* it exits from other forms of longevity risk pre-retirement. This it has done by raising the state retirement age to 68.

"One possible limited role for Government may, however, be worth consideration: the absorption of the 'extreme tail' of longevity risk post-retirement, i.e., uncertainty about the mortality experience of the minority of people who live to very old ages, say, beyond 90 or beyond 95."

(*Source*: Second report of the Pensions Commission, November 30, 2005, p. 229)

UK Insurance Industry Working Group

"Against this background, the Government could issue longevity bonds to help pension fund and annuity providers hedge the aggregate longevity risks they face, particularly for the long-tail risks associated with people living beyond age 90."

"By kick-starting this market, the Government would help provide a market-determined price for longevity risk, which could be used to help establish the optimal level of capital for the Solvency II regime of prudential regulation."

(*Source*: "Vision for the insurance industry in 2020: A report from the Insurance Industry Working Group." July 2009)

Confederation of British Industry (CBI)

"Government should press ahead with changes that make it more possible for schemes to adapt to changing circumstances—for instance [...] seeding a market for products that help firms manage their liabilities, like longevity bonds."

"Government should drive development of a market in longevity bonds, a similar instrument to annuities, by which the payments on the bonds depend on the proportion of a reference population that is still surviving at the date of payment of each coupon. This should be done through limited seed capital and supporting policy work on the topic. Government could also consider how best to match government bond issues to pension scheme needs, including the provision of more long-dated bonds and whether government should issue mortality bonds itself."

(*Source*: "Redressing the balance: Boosting the economy and protecting pensions." CBI brief. May 2009)

Organisation for Economic Co-operation and Development

"Governments could improve the market for annuities by issuing longevity indexed bonds and by producing a longevity index."

(*Source*: Antolin, P., and H. Blommestein. "Governments and the market for longevity-indexed bonds." OECD working paper on insurance and private pensions no. 4. January 2007)

World Economic Forum

"Given the ongoing shift towards defined contribution pension arrangements, there will be a growing need for annuities to enhance the security of retirement income. Longevity-Indexed Bonds and markets for hedging longevity risk would therefore play a critical role in ensuring an adequate provision of annuities."

(*Source*: World Economic Forum: Financing demographic shifts project, June 2009)

International Monetary Fund

"Although the private sector will further develop market-based transfer mechanisms for longevity risk if it recognizes the benefits of doing so, the government has a potential role in supporting this market. Measures could include provision of better longevity data, better regulation and supervision, and education to promote awareness of longevity risk. Those governments that are able to limit their own longevity risk could consider issuing a limited quantity of longevity bonds to jumpstart the market."

(*Source*: "The financial impact of longevity risk." Chapter 4 of *Global Financial Stability Report*, IMF, April 2012)

More Info

Articles:

Blake, David, and William Burrows. "Survivor bonds: Helping to hedge mortality risk." *Journal of Risk and Insurance* 68:2 (June 2001): 339–348. Online at: www.jstor.org/stable/2678106

Blake, David, Tom Boardman, and Andrew Cairns. "Sharing longevity risk: Why governments should issue longevity bonds." Discussion paper PI-1002. Pensions Institute/Cass Business School, February 18, 2013. Online at: pensions-institute.org/workingpapers/wp1002.pdf

Blake, David, Andrew J. G. Cairns, and Kevin Dowd. "Living with mortality: Longevity bonds and other mortality-linked securities." *British Actuarial Journal* 12:1 (March 2006): 153–228. Online at: tinyurl.com/lepm9c9 [PDF].

Cairns, Andrew J. G., David Blake, and Kevin Dowd. "A two-factor model for stochastic mortality with parameter uncertainty: Theory and calibration." *Journal of Risk and Insurance* 73:4 (December 2006): 687–718. Earlier version online at: www.pensions-institute.org/workingpapers/wp0611.pdf

Dowd, Kevin. "Survivor bonds: A comment on Blake and Burrows." *Journal of Risk and Insurance* 70:2 (June 2003): 339–348. Online at: dx.doi.org/10.1111/1539-6975.00063

1   For a Pensions Institute discussion paper written by the authors in which the case presented here is argued in more depth, see Blake, Boardman, and Cairns (2013).

2   It is also possible that the trend of life expectancy could decline, due to factors such as obesity and environmental degradation.

3   The situation is particularly acute for insurance companies operating in the European Union, where a new regulatory regime, Solvency II, is due to be introduced in 2014. The current Solvency II proposals, if adopted, will require insurers to hold significant additional capital (believed by many to be greater than the economic capital level) to back their annuity liabilities if longevity risk cannot be hedged effectively or marked to market.

4   The model was estimated from an application of the Cairns, Blake, and Dowd (2006) mortality model to data for the period 1991 to 2006.

5   The final coupon incorporates a terminal payment equal to the discounted value of the sum of the post-105 survivor rates to account for those who survive beyond age 105. The terminal payment is calculated on the maturity date of the bond and will depend on the numbers of the cohort who are still alive at that time and on projections of their remaining survivorship. It is intended to avoid the payment of trivial sums at very high ages.

6   One reason for this is that pension plans and annuity books have far fewer members than the national population. They will experience random variation in their mortality rates, even though they had the same mortality profile at the outset. Another reason is that most pension plans and annuity books will not have the same mortality profile as the national population. Mortality rates vary by socioeconomic status, and there have also been persistent socioeconomic variations in the rate of decline. Some commentators regard basis risk in longevity risk hedging as a big issue. However, it seems to be much less important in other risk management areas, such as interest rate hedging, where the key issue is to get the hedge in place quickly to avoid potential losses, rather than ensuring that the hedge is perfect.

7   The first suggestion that governments do this was made in 2001 (Blake and Burrows, 2001).

8   An increasing number of organizations have begun to recognize government involvement in a longevity bond market as potentially useful; see the Appendix for details.

9   This is the two-dimensional plot, with future years along the vertical axis and age along the horizontal axis, which shows the market-determined longevity risk premium at each age for each future year. It is analogous to the term structure of interest rates, which is a plot of interest rates for each future year.

10 Pension plans and annuity providers might still be willing to invest in government-issued longevity bonds covering the age range 65–90 if they are competitively priced compared with capital market hedges.

11 Governments throughout the world are beginning to do this in any case and will have to continue doing so if longevity continues to improve.

Climate Change and Alternative Risk Financing: Adapting Current Methods for Assessing and Transferring Weather Risks[1]

by Alex Bernhardt, Tanya Havlicek, and Neal Drawas

This Chapter Covers

- Climate change is having a recognized and evolving impact on local weather patterns, vulnerable individuals, and global businesses.

- Current probabilistic weather risk models used to evaluate a variety of risk management decisions are based largely upon historical data and do not adequately account for the likely future effects of climate change.

- Relatively large shifts in hazard distributions, such as those being engendered by climate change for certain weather risks, may cause such models to fail.

- In order to better account for the impacts of climate change and to continue to present reasonably accurate risk assessments, the next generation of weather risk models needs to evolve. This will entail the incorporation of new modeling techniques based on interdisciplinary methods, synthetic/modified datasets, and "big data" climate inputs to improve their adaptive capacity.

- Until models improve, risk managers and underwriters must recognize the possibility of model failure and decide what approach is best at predicting the impact of climate change based on specific scenario, exposure type, and duration.

- In the meantime, risk managers have access to a number of viable risk financing options which can diminish the volatility of their weather-related risks. Specifically index-based or parametric risk transfer solutions can be designed to protect both tangible (e.g. owned buildings) and intangible (e.g. supply chain) exposures which would otherwise be difficult or expensive to insure on a traditional indemnity basis due to gaps in the availability of relevant probabilistic models.

Introduction

Climate experts use scientific principles to correlate the Earth's thermal balance with known historical atmospheric conditions (e.g. greenhouse gas (GHG) concentrations) and then use statistical principles to extrapolate climate change processes. From this basis they are able to simulate and project specific reproductions of the observed features of historical climate change into the future using "four-dimensional" modeling software run on supercomputers. From these complex model simulations and underlying scientific research, we have learned that the climate is indeed changing and in diverse and potentially catastrophic ways. As stated by Curry, Weaver, and Wiebe (2012):

- global mean surface temperatures have risen by three-quarters of a degree Celsius over the last 100 years (1906–2005) (see Figure 1 for broader historical context highlighting the significance of this temporal shift);

- the surface temperature warming rate for the last 50 years has been approximately twice the rate for the last 100 years;

- the 16 warmest years on record since 1950 occurred in the 17-year period from 1995 to 2011;

- over the past two decades, the global average sea level has been rising at a rate of approximately 3 mm per year versus an average of 1.7–1.8 mm per year throughout the 20th century;[2]

- increased heating at the Earth's surface increases evaporation especially over the oceans, and thus enhances the moisture-holding capacity of the atmosphere at a rate of about 7% per degree centigrade.[3]

Many of the above-mentioned data are based on global averages; however, the global climate is an extremely complex system and, depending on the region observed, changes in climate variables can be significantly higher or lower than the global average. For example, the rate of sea-level rise (SLR) in the southwestern Pacific Ocean, the location of numerous low-lying island communities, is almost four times the global mean value. The resulting impacts of climate change on people and assets have manifested through the changing frequency and severity of regional hydro-meteorological perils, including droughts, floods, wildfires, extreme temperature, and storms of all types.

Figure 1. Instrumental and proxy climate evidence of the variations in average large-scale surface temperatures in the Northern Hemisphere over the last 1300 years. (a) Various annual mean instrumental temperature records. (b) Some reconstructions using multiple climate proxy records. (c) Overlap of the published multidecadal time-scale uncertainty ranges of all temperature reconstructions. (*Source:* Solomon *et al.*, 2007, Figure 6.10)

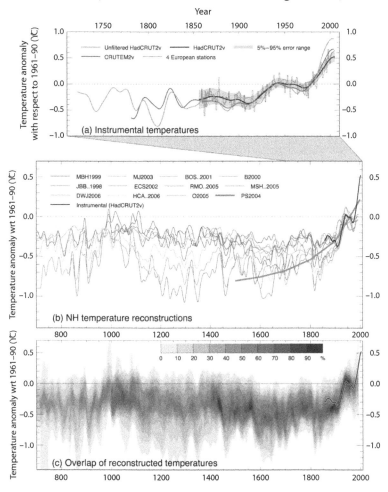

Given regional variability, characterizing and assessing the potential impacts of climate change on "at-risk" entities, whether insured or not, is a complex quest. So how then does an an individual business, or public entity assess the probability and magnitude of its risks associated with climate change? The appropriate response to this question would be an equivocal: "it depends"...on a variety of factors, including the spatial and temporal scales that characterize the entity's risk profile and exposure, the criteria by which the entity's vulnerability is valued, and the level of certainty desired for such valuations.

Historically, when contemplating financial risks, industry management did not typically incorporate environmental risks as relevant into its business planning—these concerns instead were relegated to academia, to government, and to specialized risk mitigation providers that represented a fraction of the risk management industry. If we agree with the widely held consensus that the climate is indeed changing, then we should expand our focus and consider that such changes will have significant risk management implications, affecting each business in different ways, within different time frames, and at varying financial magnitudes. Climate change will affect every business and public entity that is susceptible directly or indirectly to weather variability and, in turn, will influence the design of risk- and loss-projection models used for resource and risk management decision-making. The insurance and reinsurance industry, in its critical role as society's aggregator and distributor of risk, thus finds itself at the nexus of a suite of challenges posed by a shifting and unknown risk landscape due to climate change. Evidencing the extent of this challenge is the increasing frequency and severity of extreme weather events and related economic and insured losses worldwide, as seen in Figures 2 and 3.

Figure 2. The difference between economic and insured weather catastrophe losses worldwide 1980–2012. (*Source*: Münchener Rückversicherungs-Gesellschaft, Geo Risks Research, NatCat-SERVICE, as at January 2013)

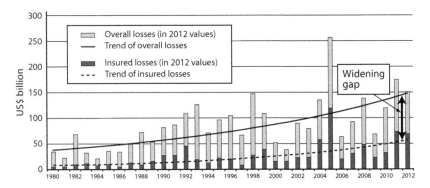

Figure 3. The number of weather catastrophe events occurring worldwide 1980–2012. (*Source*: As Figure 2)

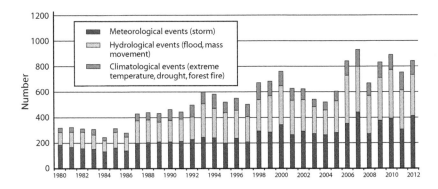

Commentary on observations from property insurers provides insight into general classes of topics and questions that risk industry professionals need to consider when characterizing exposures to climate change. To start from the most basic precepts, property is valued using one of many methods and, depending on the location of the property, its value can be imperiled by any of a variety of extreme weather phenomena. A property owner can choose to "self-insure" and pay directly financial and other property losses due to perils as they occur, or to transfer his/her risk by purchasing an insurance policy.[4] Integral to the pricing of any risk transfer product is a statistical model that predicts future losses in accordance with the associated promise of risk mitigation. Any modeled risk then has a hazard or loss function to predict future losses as accurately as possible based largely on past loss results. However, risk modelers must be cognizant of likely future shifts in the risk hazard and exposure concentrations which will change the insured entity's overall risk profile.

Existing statistical models do not include all potential interactions between assets and hazards; however, for loss models to be useful, they must adequately capture the key processes and feedbacks that affect their output. Increases in the mean and variance of the frequency and severity of extreme weather events affect the hazard input parameters of property insurance models. To capture the possible effects of climate change on hurricane incidence and strength in the United States, many of the major vendors of catastrophe models, including AIR Worldwide, EQECAT, and RMS, have developed models using two different underlying event sets: one extrapolated from the full historical record and the other from more recent events that have taken place when Atlantic sea surface temperatures have been higher than the long-term average. The latter type of model is intended to better reflect the effects of near-term climatic trends than the model based on the longer historical event set. Box 1 gives more detail.

Box 1. Statement by RMS Explaining Rationale for Developing "Short-Term" US Hurricane Model

"Hurricane activity responds to warm sea surface temperatures (SSTs), which have been above the long-term historical average since the early 1990s. While the debate about the cause of increased SSTs continues, there is scientific consensus that the proportion of intense hurricanes (Category 3–5) has increased and that overall hurricane frequency has been significantly higher than the long-term historical average since 1995. The annual average of category 1–5 hurricanes making first landfalls along the U.S. coastline from 1970 to 1994 is close to 1.3, while since 1995 it is around 2.0 per year. Therefore, most hurricane experts believe that simply using the long-term historical average number of hurricanes is not the best way to estimate future activity."

(*Source*: Risk Market News, 2010).

How should decision-makers incorporate or react to such information on apparent climate change? Among responses are to withdraw from the market or to increase deductibles in areas with higher or more volatile than expected losses, both of which can impact insurance supply and demand and create societal risk mitigation problems if coverage becomes unavailable or unaffordable.

Problem Definition: Matching Hazards to Exposures

To address the broader question of how climate change is affecting the insurance industry and other climate-vulnerable entities requires an understanding of the current state of climate science and its application to risk models. The scientific method strives to achieve and ensure impartiality, an aim that is bolstered by a technical peer-review process for publications before they are disseminated. Again, climate experts use scientific principles and known historical data to correlate the Earth's thermal balance with historically known quantities, such as GHG concentrations in the atmosphere. By considering various industrial emission scenarios and making assumptions about future socioeconomic variables (e.g. population, economic policies, and technological development), the climate change models that generate defensible predictions as informed by observed historical changes facilitate an exploration of possible future states of the climate system. Current global climate models are projecting a continuation of recent historical trends in climate variables.

Of specific concern to insurers and risk managers are (Curry, Weaver, and Wiebe, 2012):

• accelerating losses of ice and snow over land and thermal expansion of the oceans, which contribute to sea level rise, which in turn alters the frequency and severity of coastal flooding and storm surges;

- an overall strengthening of the hydrological cycle, leading to precipitation increases at mid-to high latitudes and decreases in low latitudes;

- an increase in the frequency of heat extremes, and increased frequency of drought in normally dry regions and extreme rainfall in normally wet regions;

- a rise in the frequency and average intensity of tropical cyclones, increasing their destructive potential.

Potential direct and indirect impacts to entities from the observed and projected changes in climate variables are complex and include changes in morbidity and mortality trends and less predictable damage to property (including agricultural products) from floods, drought, wildfires, and strong storms. Meteorological shifts affect both environmental and economic ecosystems—the global economy will be affected by alterations in the demand for adaptive management strategies. They also create challenges for natural resource management, for example in fisheries, mining, water supply, forestry, and agriculture. For companies which invest in or rely on these natural resource commodities, unstable resource availability and financial risks are present on both the asset and liability side of their balance sheets.

Beyond simply identifying a list of potential disasters, disruptions, and potential financial losses due to climate change, there are a number of risk management questions. Are these risks avoidable, manageable, or transferable? Are they already contained in existing insurance policies and risk management procedures? If so, what happens to these policies and procedures when the risks change? How do you insure or otherwise mitigate systemic or covariant risks? (That is, decision-making here requires an understanding of existing and potential correlations and depends by and large on the extent of risk diversification.) What alternative risk mitigation strategies are available for traditionally uninsurable risks? Are the risks relevant for decision-making now—or are the expected effects too remote in time, space, or perceived significance? (For example, perhaps discounting makes the net present effect undetectable.) To best answer these questions the (re)insurance industry turns to risk modeling.

Models and Surprise

Using insurance risk management mechanisms as an example, if the expected loss and volatility components of an insurance premium are incorrectly priced, the actual performance of the insurance product and the modeled expectations for it will deviate from one another more than anticipated—which may cause unpleasant surprises for an insurer or an insured. Mispricing can have unpleasant consequences, and a major cause of mispricing is model error. Unexpected deviations in hazards—which can manifest as unanticipated losses to the insurer or reveal systematic overpricing of risk to a consumer—must be judged, and risk modelers and managers must decide if such deviations are tolerable or whether adjustments to the risk transfer product are required to accommodate them, for example in the form of a rate increase/decrease or a change in policy structure. Marginal adjustments like these are sufficient when shifts are similar in scale to the loss variable, such as inflation. But relatively large shifts in the hazard distribution, such as those being engendered by climate change, tend to cause risk models to fail.

Another unforeseeable effect is when unanticipated liabilities become covered under an existing policy, as was the case with asbestos. Potentially, damages due to GHG emissions may be covered under certain pollution liability policies that were not intended or priced to include GHG liabilities. Up to this time, courts in the United States have found that GHG emitters and their insurers are not liable for claims for damages due to climate change,[5] though this could yet change.

Box 2. Decisive Action in a Climate of Uncertainty

"As the consensus that the [sic] climate change is becoming more evident grows, data across many disciplines (including forestry, water and land management, for example) remains limited, not readily available or communicated in a format that might not facilitate actionable decisions on climate adaptation. Yet, future climate risks may require human judgement today or in the coming years, while the full scientific data may not come until it is too late. Complex systems such as the climate are non-linear by nature— chain reactions through the system are unpredictable and not directly proportional to the size of the triggers. A limited amount of data and constraints on computational power have been strong impediments to bringing greater clarity into predicting future climatic developments at a local level...

"Faced with uncertainty about the likely effectiveness and risk of unintended consequences of a proposed intervention, policy-makers can be paralyzed by a desire to wait for more detailed analyses and data regarding the precise timing, manifestation or impact of future climatic changes in their local environments. Greater support for scientific research, better computational power and data are needed to shed greater clarity into predicting future climatic developments, especially the climate and weather extremes."

(*Source*: World Economic Forum report "Global risks 2013." Howell (2013))

The current state of climate risk management for organizations and individuals is that making strategic or operational decisions about mitigating risk which will affect short-, medium-, and long-term outcomes is done in an environment with little exacting information and high uncertainty about potential shifts in short-, medium-, and long-term circumstance due to climate change. How this challenge will specifically affect different risk sectors will be unique and will depend on the temporal and spatial scale of their operations (e.g. just how long is long-term?); however, the general problem is shared (see Box 2). This is a situation that is distinct from making decisions with information uncertainty in a stable equilibrium, which needs only consider stochasticity and tail events within a stable distribution and not a fundamental shift of the underlying distribution. As illustrated in Figures 2 and 3, the mean and volatility in the number of natural disasters was greater in the 2000s than in the 1980s. The critical risk modeling question is whether a shift has occurred in the distribution of extreme events or whether the observed values are all part of the same distribution. If the observed events are all part of the same distribution, is that distribution properly described in current risk management models? While approaches to address this dilemma are not mutually exclusive, model factors are fundamentally different depending on the understanding of the underlying phenomena.

The pivotal question is whether you believe natural disasters are in a stable equilibrium, or natural events occur in a continuously shifting landscape. The models used to explore these climatic states are distinct as they allow for different possible outcomes and require different model-fitting procedures. Each risk manager and modeler must address this question and decide which approach is better at predicting the impact of climate change for each specific scenario, exposure type, and duration. Practically, this will entail the utilization of new sophisticated modeling techniques based on interdisciplinary methods, synthetic datasets, and/or the incorporation of "big data" climate inputs to better adapt to the variable effects of ongoing changes. Figure 4 shows how climate change and modeling itself may be influenced by externalities such as climate emission policies. However, even modeling future global temperature fluctuations is a magnitude less complicated than extrapolating the likely future effects of a changing global temperature on, say, local property losses.

Figure 4. Predictions of Intergovernmental Panel on Climate Change (IPCC) global surface temperature model given certain scenarios. The mean outcomes for each scenario are denoted by the thick lines. The uncertainty surrounding each mean scenario (+/– 1 sigma) is shown by the shaded areas. Note: the uncertainty around any multimodel approach to surface temperature prediction will be compounded by the uncertainty associated with scenario outcomes, which will be influenced by difficult-to-predict human factors such as public policy and individual behavior. (*Source*: Mandia (2012), adapted from Solomon *et al.* (2007, Fig. 10.4))

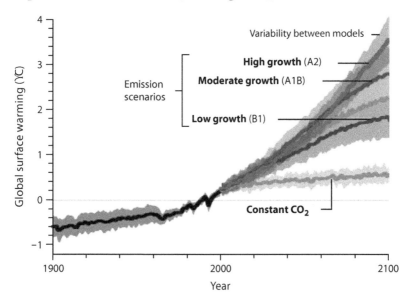

Of specific concern for risk managers and modelers with respect to climate change and extreme events is a systematic underestimation of the frequency, severity, and volatility of events due to unaccounted for shifts in the "upper-level" hazard functions that cause loss. Chronic underestimation of loss or its volatility will produce negative insurance coverage results. These issues are succinctly summarized, in descending order, as assumption risk, model risk, parameter risk, and process risk. Assumption risk occurs due to violations of one or more assumptions associated with the model, and these assumptions may be implicit or explicit. The risk that the model used does not concur with the modeled system of interest is a model risk. Parameter risk arises when the estimated parameters of the model are incorrect or when parameters shift over the time frame of system behavior. Process risk is associated with the stochastic behavior which the system exhibits as compared to the expected value the model predicts.

Consider the possibility of a changing storm peril that leads to higher than expected losses with more uncertainty. Suppose that thunderstorm frequency and severity are modeled as a stable average that does not increase over time and exhibits only modest variability. But in fact the actual thunderstorm frequency and severity show behavior that is more similar to an increasing linear trend with increasing variation. The conflict is in the deviation between model expectations of system dynamics, the actual dynamics exhibited by the system (what is experienced), and the ability of the modeler to detect differences between actual and expected, including changes in loss volatility versus model error.

Although there is not a universal solution to these issues, there are many parameters and constraints to consider in decision-making with respect to both problem definition and solution development. In addition to expected losses due to extreme weather is the temporal scale on which expected returns are measured and the amount of perceived volatility that can be incorporated into the contingencies provision of a risk price. Irrespective of a given model's results, regulations and other societal goals can prevent insurers from achieving required price increases or coverage restrictions even if pricing models have suggested that there should be rate increases or market withdrawal because of eroding performance. The market availability of reinsurance and other catastrophe risk management products, as well as policy structure such as the size of deductibles, determine the options available. The influence of reinsurance pricing and capacity in particular on the fluidity of catastrophe risk transfer markets is evidenced by the high percentage of insured catastrophe losses ultimately borne by reinsurers (see Figure 5 for several recent examples). These are just some of the issues which risk managers must consider to assess adequately their exposures and risk mitigation responses to the expected physical effects of climate change.

Figure 5. Many major catastrophe events tend to be ultimately paid for by reinsurers. (*Source*: Insurance Information Institute, from reinsurance-share percentages provided in press release by Royal Automobile Association of South Australia (RAA), Association of Bermudan Insurers and Reinsurers (ABIR), and Comité Européen des Assurances (CEA) dated January 13, 2011; economic loss figures from EM-DAT, the emergency events database maintained by the Centre for Research on the Epidemiology of Disasters (CRED))

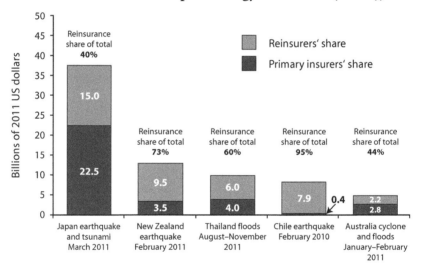

Climate Change and Risk Transfer Markets

The climate is a dynamic and kinetic system and the course of its change is difficult to track despite the tremendous amount of research and computing power that is directed at the issue. The complexity of such a system makes its effects on specific weather perils sufficiently inscrutable as to undermine both potential supply and demand for related risk transfer products. Uncertainty makes insurance markets wary, and an overriding concern for more tangible and immediate risks consumes the potential beneficiaries of weather risk transfer. This means that a market whose sole function would be climate change insurance *per se* has yet to develop.

This is unfortunate considering the dramatic effects that climate change appears to have both on specific market segments and on the global economy as a whole, as evidenced by the rising economic impact of natural disasters. Figure 2 shows a trend toward more severe loss activity than even the record levels exhibited in the past three decades. It also illustrates (along with the specific event examples featured in Figure 6) the widening gap between economic and insured losses which, if unchecked, will result in significant social problems as a consequence of the fact that uninsured catastrophe losses are inevitably borne by unaffected third parties (e.g. governments and their citizen/corporate taxpayers). Although these loss figures may have been inflated to some extent by demographic trends acting in parallel to climate change, such as coastal urbanization and broad-based economic development, climate change risks are clearly significant factors affecting such growth. This is highlighted by Figure 3, which shows a dramatic trend toward a higher overall frequency of weather-driven catastrophes.

Figure 6. In many cases economic losses far outstrip (re)insured losses. (*Source*: As Figure 5)

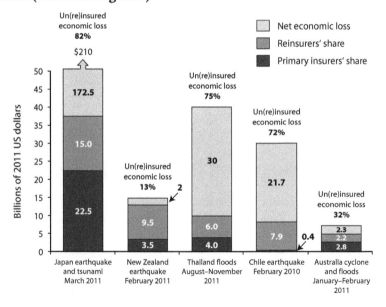

Irrespective of its causes, climate change is a reality with significant financial implications for individuals, corporations, (re)insurers, and governments. Efforts to mitigate the adverse effects of changing climate, though necessary, are too little too late as far as prudent financial risk management is concerned. Considering the latent effects of carbon dioxide and other GHGs on atmospheric conditions, even putting an absolute stop to emissions today would only serve to partially abate, not halt, the process of change (Curry, Weaver, and Wiebe, 2012). So if climate change mitigation is only a partial solution, from a practical perspective we must prepare simultaneously to adapt. It is increasingly clear that without concerted adaptive action, current loss trends threaten to undermine fiscally a number of significant personal, commercial, and social endeavors.

The potentially positive news is that weather-related risks are by and large insurable despite the current debate around the efficacy of models. As the present effects of climate change are experienced in the form of ever more extreme and unpredictable weather patterns, and as its potential long-term effects are continually documented and debated, awareness is building of the increasing exposure to weather risk of governments, corporations, and individuals. Such attention has served in recent years to increase the awareness of alternative risk transfer products.

However, awareness has not yet translated into concerted action—as evidenced by the growing worldwide gap between economic and insured weather catastrophe losses (as emphasized by the arrow in Figure 2). The impact of this gap on local and regional economies can be profound. Figure 6 highlights the economic losses that have resulted from several recent major catastrophes, including the floods in Thailand of 2011. This event was more than 70% un(re)insured, resulting in a total liability of US$30 billion—more than 8% of the country's gross domestic product (GDP) that year. Overall, this hit caused a 9% decline in Thailand's GDP in the last three months of 2011 compared to the year before and led to the economy growing by just 0.1% for the full year.[6]

Delving a bit deeper into the dynamics that influence such gaps reveals an unforeseen threat to global economic sustainability and security.

While most insured losses are accounted for by events that affect the developed world, uninsured losses are incurred and retained disproportionately by developing world markets where the majority of the population is low-income and the professional risk transfer industry is less robust. Developed world organizations with global supply chains suffer from the adverse effects of catastrophe losses that occur downstream largely in the form of supply chain disruption or (contingent) business interruption.

In these markets it is difficult to fill the gap using traditional or developed-world means for several reasons. Primarily, the data landscape and risk modeling foundation for indemnity-based catastrophe insurance in developing markets tends to be more remedial (or in certain instances nonexistent), rendering some risks uninsurable— without a probabilistic risk model which produces results somewhere within the bounds of "reasonable uncertainty," commercial underwriters understandably cannot commit capital. The same adage holds true for more intangible first-party exposures such as supply chain or business interruption, for which reliable modeling techniques are equally difficult. Moreover, the challenge of insuring the global poor cannot be achieved simply by downscaling traditional products; hence the advent and precipitous growth of the modern microinsurance market, which has employed a host of product and business model innovations to date.[7]

For the insurance of low-income groups, or of difficult-to-understand and quantify and/or very large risk exposures (or portfolios thereof) against catastrophic weather risks, one of the most promising current approaches involves the use of index-based or parametric risk transfer solutions. An index-based risk transfer product relies on the determination of an external parameter for loss calculation, such as windspeed or rainfall, rather than on the relatively subjective assessment of actual property damage incurred post loss. Data for the design of such products can come from a variety of ground-based (e.g. weather station) or remote-sensed (e.g. satellite) sources. From the perspective of (re)insurers, such products are relatively easy to model and underwrite since they require a detailed understanding only of the covered hazard and are impartial as to that hazard's effect on the risk it is designed to protect. This eliminates a layer of uncertainty from the underwriting process.

Such products are also relatively easy and cost-effective to administer since they eliminate the need for loss adjustors, minimize the risk of moral hazard, and provide purchasers with quick payouts in the event of loss. However, unlike traditional indemnity-based solutions, such products do not provide a perfect hedge against the actual experience of the insured, introducing them to basis risk, or the risk of mismatch between a parametric payout and actual associated losses.

Index-based risk transfer solutions offer (re)insurers and other risk transfer counterparties (e.g. capital markets players) the ability to underwrite risk objectively and, subject to the appropriate management of or disregard for basis risk, can help clients to minimize their exposure to loss due to catastrophe. The global braintrust for the analysis and commercial underwriting of catastrophe risk resides primarily in the reinsurance market, where much of the insured losses from catastrophes ultimately reside. This is evidenced by the high percentage of insured losses retained by reinsurers in recent events, including several from 2011, the worst year for cumulative economic losses from catastrophes on record (Figure 5).

Given the reinsurance industry's highly sophisticated understanding of catastrophe risk and the increasing volatility of certain hazards, reinsurers have been some of the most ardent adopters of parametric risk transfer solutions both as sponsors and as risk-bearing counterparties. Most often such solutions are used to hedge peak risks and are supported by so-called alternative capacity, a distinction which encapsulates a variety of heretofore exotic risk transfer vehicles such as catastrophe bonds, industry loss warranties, and sidecars. Alternative capacity represents only 14% of the approximately US$313 billion catastrophe reinsurance market as of June 1, 2013,[8] though this is nearly double the proportion in 2008 and according to most practitioners this share is projected to increase as the reinsurance and capital markets continue to converge (Figure 7).

Figure 7. Growth of alternative capacity in the property catastrophe reinsurance market over time. (*Source*: Guy Carpenter & Company, LLC)

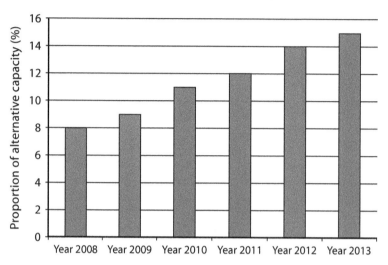

In addition to the parametric solutions that are utilized extensively by providers of alternative catastrophe reinsurance products, the weather-derivatives market, which mainly serves non-(re)insurance corporations and to date has focused on the energy sector, represents an additional approximately US$12 billion of parametric risk capacity (Brewer, 2012). While most of this risk transfer product is purchased by energy companies in developed world markets, a growing share of weather-related transactions is being developed and deployed in other sectors, such as agriculture, food and beverages, apparel, and financial services. However, it is fair to say that the (re)insurance and weather-derivative markets have only scratched the surface of the potential uses for parametric risk financing solutions.

There is also some significant index-based insurance activity in the microinsurance market, where innumerable pilot programs employing weather indexes have been initiated in recent years to address one of the primary risks that adversely affect the economic development of smallholder farmers and microentrepreneurs.[9] All of these separate, though related, market movements are growing in prominence, and together with adequate investment in research and resources will serve to gradually minimize the entry of uninsured catastrophe losses into the global economic system at all levels—governmental, institutional, and individual. Fostering the growth of these markets through supra- and subnational advocacy, public–private partnerships, and shareholder activism will be essential to efforts to adapt to global climate change since no more compelling mechanisms exist today for the management and financing of otherwise uninsurable catastrophic weather risk.

Conclusions

According to climate scientists, climate change is altering the historical frequency and severity of weather events. The inability to predict losses within a changing hazard landscape can have significant implications that may give rise to abrupt or irreversible impacts—for example insolvency at the company level. Many risk models assume a constant relative growth of losses, a faulty assumption in the face of constantly changing hazards. In general, any risk model must assume some window of stability over which to estimate the constant parameters present in its equations. However, the apparent or relevant instability of loss is specific to each at-risk industry sector and is dependent on the location and type of its specific exposures, the time span over which actual loss is potentially realized, and the adaptability and responsiveness of the risk models used to assess exposure and loss.

The framework for resolution of this conundrum in a changing environment is to modify the assumptions used in traditional models or create new models. Special attention must be paid to changes in the mixes of data within the past and between the past and the future. Trending and on-leveling may be able to partially overcome some issues at some scales, addressing both model and parameter risk. Alternatively, new classes of models need to be developed that are adequate to address change using interdisciplinary approaches and/or more robust data sources.

In the short term, as risk assessment methods are being adapted and improved to account for climate change, risk managers have access to a number of viable risk financing options which can diminish the volatility of weather risk. Specifically, risk transfer markets appear to be willing to assume weather risk so long as it can be adequately underwritten. Absent the advent of catastrophe models and business models which can account for and administer risks on an indemnity basis in developing world markets, the best way to finance presently uninsured catastrophic weather risks is through their parameterization. Although index-based risk transfer solutions are not a universal fix for efforts to adapt to global climate change, when coupled with targeted disaster risk-reduction efforts and increasingly lucid climate modeling techniques, some significant short-term gains will result in the form of more responsive and sustainable risk management practices and access to lower-cost capital after weather disasters.

More Info

Book:

Solomon, S., D. Qin, M. Manning, Z. Chen, M. Marquis, K. B. Averyt, M. Tignor, and H. L. Miller (eds). Climate Change 2007—The Physical Science Basis: Contribution of Working Group I to the Fourth Assessment Report of the IPCC. Cambridge, UK: Cambridge University Press, 2007. Online at: tinyurl.com/yaa3qrs

Articles:

Browne, Luke. "Thailand economy shrinks 9% on flood impact." *GlobalPost* (February 20, 2012). Online at: tinyurl.com/mgbwaky

Mandia, Scott. "Global warming isn't tomorrow—It is now." *Global Warming: Man or Myth* blog (August 5, 2012). Online at: tinyurl.com/n8hvawn

RiskMarketNews. "RMS calls criticism 'a fundamental misunderstanding' of CAT models." January 21, 2010. Online at: tinyurl.com/lpjahyj

Reports:

Brewer, Peter. "Weather markets 1.0 overview: History, acronyms and terminology, and overview." Cumulus Fahrenheit Fund Weather Markets Webinar 1.0. March 22, 2012. Online at: wrma.org/weather-markets-webinar.html

Curry, Charles, Andrew Weaver, and Ed Wiebe. "Determining the impact of climate change on insurance risk and the global community. Phase I: Key climate indicators." Solterra Solutions. November 2012. Online at: www.casact.org/research/ClimateChangeRpt_Final.pdf

Hazell, P., J. Anderson, N. Balzer, A. Hastrup Clemmensen, U. Hess, and F. Rispoli. "The potential for scale and sustainability in weather index insurance for agriculture and rural livelihoods." International Fund for Agricultural Development and World Food Programme. March 2010. Online at: www.ifad.org/ruralfinance/pub/weather.pdf

Howell, Lee (ed). "Global risks 2013." 8th ed. World Economic Forum, 2013. Online at: www3.weforum.org/docs/WEF_GlobalRisks_Report_2013.pdf

1 The authors would like to acknowledge Dr Imelda Powers and Peter Wei, CFA, ASA, for their keen editorial insights.

2 Sea level rise is attributed to both the volumetric expansion of sea water with increased temperatures and the melting of land ice, also due to increased temperatures.

3 As predicted by underlying theory (the Clausius–Clapeyron relation) and in close accord with observations. Also see Solomon *et al.* (2007), Chapter 3.4.2.

4 The property owner of course has other options at his/her disposal, including risk avoidance (e.g. sell the property) and risk control (e.g. strengthen the building against high winds), though for the purposes of this scenario we presume that the risk cannot be avoided, and disaster risk reduction falls outside the scope of this chapter.

5 Although no individual organizations have been found liable as yet, several "climate change lawsuits" have been filed to date, most notably by public entities against energy firms—see Kivalina v. ExxonMobil Corporation, *et al.*, for a prominent example (a summary can be found in Wikipedia).

6 The Thailand National Economic and Social Development Board (NESDB: www.nesdb.go.th), as referenced in Browne (2012).

7 See Microinsurance Compendiums I and II for more background on the origins, basics, and growth of microinsurance: tinyurl.com/llkqt7c

8 Guy Carpenter & Company, LLC, June 1, 2013, reinsurance renewals briefing as summarized on GCCapitalIdeas.com: tinyurl.com/k3ue2m5 and tinyurl.com/mugj5a2

9 For a good overview of weather index microinsurance programs for agriculture worldwide, see Hazell *et al.* (2010).

Climate Change and Insurance

by Stephen Haddrill

This Chapter Covers
- A discussion of the likely impact of climate change.
- The scenario 50 years on.
- Present responses to extreme weather.
- Insurance sector agreements with government.
- The limits to insurance.

Introduction

Starting from the fact that climate change is a reality that is happening now, and that we can see its impact across the world, what role does the insurance sector have in covering this? There is no doubt that climate change is of enormous importance to the insurance industry. The costs of flooding, wind damage, and abnormal heat are all huge, and climate change threatens to increase all those costs.

Work done so far on climate change shows the threat has arrived. The carbon produced in the last century is already causing extreme weather. The scientific consensus is that flooding has increased in severity due to sea level rises and more rain. Windstorms are fiercer. Heat waves are more intense. Again, the scientific consensus is that reducing carbon emissions will not reverse this trend for decades. More extreme views, such as that by the founder of Gaia theory, James Lovelock, argue that we have probably already gone past the point of no return, but this pessimistic approach is not mainstream thinking. What is clear is that both the insurance sector and the world at large have to adapt and look to protect themselves.

Failure to adapt will generate extreme economic costs. Even relatively low percentage increases in weather phenomena, such as the footprint of a flood area, lead to massively increased costs. For example, a 5% increase in the footprint of a flood can lead to a 75% increase in the consequent bill for damages.

Extreme Weather Conditions

Over the next 50 years, we expect to see:

- Windstorm losses increase by two-thirds to US$27 billion per year worldwide.

- Additional flooding costs of €100–120 billion a year in Europe.

- A 15-fold increase in UK flood costs, to £22 billion.

- Subsidence costs increasing by 50% in average clay-soil areas.

At the same time, heat stress on people, animals, machinery, and property will also increase. It is quite possible that by the 2040s, the summer of 2003 will be regarded as normal. If this becomes reality, then a quarter of working hours will be hotter than "comfort levels" in London offices, increasing the demand for air conditioning, and creating heat islands.

Floods in the United Kingdom present a good example of our concerns. While it is difficult to point to one isolated storm or flood and say conclusively, "there we have proof of climate change," the floods of 2007 nevertheless give us a picture of the effects we are facing. Torrential rain did not just lead to rivers bursting their banks. Crucially, the drains failed also, as flash flooding overwhelmed them. In all, some 180,000 people made claims, or four times the annual average of flood claimants. Another way of putting this is that the industry experienced four years' worth of claims in just two months.

At the same time, the floods put a significant percentage of the United Kingdom's infrastructure at great risk. Reservoir banks threatened to fail. The electricity supply to 600,000 homes was almost lost, and the water supply to those homes was in fact lost for a while—this despite the fact that the insurance industry has issued repeated warnings to government about the vulnerability of critical infrastructure.

The Response of Insurance Companies

To date, the insurance industry has coped with extreme weather events extremely well. In the 2007 floods in the United Kingdom, most insurers had loss adjusters on the ground within 24 hours, often calling in staff from overseas. People were put in temporary housing within days, and almost all are now back in their homes. Two hundred families were still displaced at the end of September, but virtually all because they required special building work.

There are, however, some lessons to learn. People talk to each other in a crisis. If a loss adjuster representing one insurer gives information to one household, while another gives different information to a neighbor, people get confused. The sector therefore came together to standardize the process of communicating with citizens in an afflicted area after an extreme weather event.

People in hard-hit areas worry greatly whether they will be able to obtain insurance again. The industry has been tremendously resourceful in continuing to provide insurance cover in "at-risk" areas, and it has done so at very reasonable premium prices. However, there is a need for governments around the world to be alert to the dangers of allowing building on flood plains and low-lying coastal areas in an era of rising sea levels.

Insurance covers risk. It is not there to cover loss that is absolutely certain to be incurred—you cannot insure your house once it is on fire! It is a fact that, in both America and the United Kingdom, and in many European countries, some of the most valuable properties, infrastructure assets, and concentrations of people live in areas that are going to be more at risk from tidal surges, flooding, and rising sea levels in the years and decades ahead.

The 2007 floods were the result of extreme rainfall. Water also threatens us from the seas, particularly as sea levels are expected to increase by at least a meter this century. If nothing is done, the risk of the 1953 flood being repeated will increase from 1 in 1000 in 2000, to 1 in 100 by 2100 (figures from the UK Environmental Agency).

The financial cost of a major storm on the UK east coast, for example, could reach £15–20 billion, as quoted in an Association of British Insurers (ABI) report, "Coastal flood risk—Thinking for tomorrow, acting today," published in November 2006. This is not a fantastical, or a remote possibility. In 2008, the United Kingdom was just hours away from a combination of a tidal surge, strong east winds, and high water levels in the Thames causing flooding in London, according to the London Meteorological Office. The ABI report used insurance catastrophe models to examine the effects of a rise in sea levels on flood risk.

Handling such an event would be extremely difficult. A high proportion of our emergency facilities are on the coastal flood plain. It is worth bearing in mind that the number of people over the age of 75 (the least-mobile members of our community) living on the UK coast is expected to double in the next 30 years, according to ABI research.

Taking all this together, the adaptation of homes, business, and the infrastructure economy is vital for every country. Adaptation requires concerted action at an international level, and at the national level, as well as by the global insurance industry. In the United Kingdom, over the last year, the sector has worked with the whole range of public authorities to put in place a new blueprint for the future, and good progress has been made on all sides.

International and British Strategies

First, the international dimension: There is already international action on carbon reduction. That international cooperation needs to be repeated for adaptation. Globally agreed principles need to feed into EU strategic plans. Storms do not respect borders, nor do rivers in flood. Across the European Union, we need a better understanding of risk, and we need agreement on the standard of protection required across Europe.

Such international strategies must, however, promote and encourage national and local action. Successful adaptation requires a framework that allows regional and local authorities to develop their individual action plans, responding to the specific threats affecting each locality.

The UK government has proposed new legislation to start creating this framework. We need to see two fundamental measures. First, there needs to be a commitment to a properly coordinated flood-management system in the United Kingdom, with clarity about who will be responsible for drainage. The government is talking here about a new strategic role for the Environment Agency, but the details will be critical.

Secondly, the United Kingdom and Europe need a commitment to a new, long-term, flood-management strategy, with a commitment to invest consistently over the long term. The industry needs to ensure that flood insurance remains as affordable and widely available as possible, so that consumers and small businesses can continue to be able to protect themselves from the financial cost of flooding.

Since 2000, this has been achieved in the United Kingdom through the "Statement of Principles on Flood Insurance," which commit insurers to provide flood insurance to homes that are already covered, provided the risk is not worse than 1:75, or if flood protection works are planned within five years. Under this arrangement, half a million homes at high risk of flooding have been protected. In fact, the sector is probably protecting an additional 400,000 homes that are not strictly covered by the agreement.

The statement has been a good deal for consumers in many respects, but it has not been entirely good for the market. The cost has fallen on existing insurers alone. New entrants to the market have no obligation to existing customers, and so are not affected. Specialist insurance for higher-risk customers has not developed, and because insurers have insured more people than they need to, inappropriate new property developments have secured insurance cover.

In its latest agreement with the UK government, the UK insurance industry has addressed these points. The new agreement sets out a series of government actions that are necessary to enable flood insurance to continue to be as widely available as possible in the future.

These include:

- Agreement by government to move away from a short-term, three-year approach to flood-risk management. Instead, the Environment Agency will publish a paper setting out a range of options for protecting the country over the next 25 years. This will facilitate a full debate about the best way forward. The government will then publish its response by the next spending review, setting out long-term aims and the associated funding.

- Risk data will be improved by the Environment Agency, and these will be made more readily available.

- Planning policy will be evaluated by early 2009, to ensure the new planning rules are delivering at both strategic and practical levels (it must be said that the early evidence is positive).

- Properties built from 2009 onwards are now explicitly excluded from the statement so that the onus clearly lies on developers to ensure their development is insurable.

Another important feature of this agreement is that it sets an end-date for the insurer commitments of June 30, 2013, after which what is, after all, a market distortion, will be removed. This instance shows how national governments can cooperate with the insurance industry to provide insurance, even under difficult circumstances.

However, the ABI and the industry are very keen to ensure that it is made obvious whether a new development is a good flood risk or not. We are working with the Royal Institute of Chartered Surveyors to develop a kitemark that can be applied to new homes. This will assure prospective owners whether their new home will be insurable or not. In this way, the market can be made to work for adaptation. Second, both the ABI and the industry will do more to promote better understanding of climate risk among the general population.

To this end, we will be publishing research on the economic costs of climate impacts. We will disseminate new climate data within the industry by hosting discussions among insurers and scientists about new climate science scenarios. We will also be working with government to educate the general public, by offering advice and tools for individuals to understand climate risks.

Home owners can also be encouraged to make their homes more resilient to flooding, and the ABI will produce new guidance for property developers about making new developments more climate-resilient. It will also research the cost of resilient repairs, and will continue to work with the industry and government on options for increasing the take-up of cost-effective resilience measures.

ClimateWise

Finally, the ABI is a strong supporter of the ClimateWise initiative. ClimateWise is a set of principles that commits insurers and the wider insurance industry to build climate change into their business operations. ClimateWise was developed by the UK industry, with the support of the Prince of Wales, to strengthen efforts to tackle climate change, including carrying out further research into climate change, and to promote the findings.

The insurance industry reaches into millions of homes and businesses, and has a key role to play in enabling customers to prepare for changing weather, as well as encouraging them to reduce their own emissions.

Conclusion

The UK sector has had warning of the scale of the threat. The floods of 2007 showed that new effort is needed. It did not tell us exactly what to do, nor where or how to do it. Since then the industry, and those outside the industry, have come up with many good ideas for a safer future. These ideas now need to be acted on.

More Info

Reports:
Association of British Insurers. "Coastal flood risk—Thinking of tomorrow, acting today." November 2006. Online at: tinyurl.com/m3vye9o [PDF].

Association of British Insurers. "Climate adaptation—Guidance on insurance issues for new developments." January 23, 2009. Online at: tinyurl.com/khjm7e5

Islamic Insurance Markets and the Structure of *Takaful*

by Suzanne White

This Chapter Covers

- Islamic scholars object to the concept of conventional insurance due to three key elements: *riba* (usury), *gharar* (uncertainty), and *maysir* (gambling).

- Islamic insurance or *takaful* operators have therefore redesigned their management and accounting practices to comply with *shariah* law.

- *Takaful* and conventional or traditional insurance policy wordings both operate in a similar way, with the protection that is provided to the client being exactly the same.

- The differences between Islamic and conventional insurance lie in the ownership and financing of the company, in the management and accounting systems, and in the entities in which the premiums are invested.

- Islamic insurance is a very close concept to that of "mutual insurers" in the West and, in particular, to those we call "ethical" insurers.

Introduction

Insurance plays a vital role in supporting both national and international economic development and growth. Islamic countries are no exception. The main issue for insurers in the Islamic world is that many Islamic scholars view conventional insurance as prohibited by Islam.

Muslim scholars are not against the concept of risk mitigation, risk sharing, or risk management, including risk financing, *per se*. In fact, they support the compensation of victims of misfortune. However, many scholars consider some aspects of conventional insurance contracts as being prohibited from a *shariah* (Islamic law) point of view. *Shariah* covers all aspects of a Muslim's life, not just worship.

Prohibited Factors of Insurance

Several *fatawa* (the plural of *fatwa*, meaning an answer to a question related to an issue of *shariah*) have been issued by eminent Muslim scholars on the subject of insurance. The objections tend to relate to the insurance contract itself or to insurance market practice in general.

Objections relating to the insurance contract itself are those of *riba* (usury), *gharar* (uncertainty), and *maysir* (gambling). The other objections relating to market practice are usually concerned with two issues: the first is that insurance companies' investment policies are generally interest-bearing (which is not acceptable in Islam); and the second issue is the fact that life assurance is considered to breach Islamic inheritance rules by distributing the sum assured among beneficiaries. These objections relating to market practice can be easily overcome by the insurer making changes to their company policy, as they do not affect the insurance contract itself.

The objections related to the contract itself, however, require the restructuring of insurance contracts to be in line with *shariah*.

Riba (Usury)

Under a conventional insurance contract, the insured pays the insurance company a premium (either as a lump sum in general insurance or as installments in life insurance), in exchange for financial compensation at the time of a claim, subject to the happening of an insured occurrence or event. Claims are generally larger amounts than the premium paid. Islamic law objects to this payment on the grounds that a small amount of money (premium) is being exchanged for a larger amount of money (claim). Scholars consider this an unjustified increase of money, and therefore *riba*. Islamic insurers therefore have to structure their operations and investments to avoid *riba*.

Gharar (Uncertainty)

Gharar can be defined as uncertainty or ambiguity. Islamic law seeks to avoid ambiguity in contracts in order to prevent disputes and conflict between parties. This is a general Islamic principle that must be applied to all contracts, including insurance.

In the case of conventional insurance, neither the insurer nor the insured knows the outcome of the contract (i.e. whether a loss will occur or not). The insurer is entitled to get the premium in all cases, whereas the insured may not receive a claim because the payment of claims depends on the probability of loss occurrence (which is a random variable). Other uncertain elements are as to when the claim may be paid and how much the insured may receive.

In life assurance contracts, *gharar* can be seen to exist even in the premium, as the insured party does not know how much he will pay to the insurance company each year, or for how many years. The insured may know the monthly or yearly premium, but he does not know how much he will pay to the insurer before he dies. In general insurance (nonlife insurance), the premium is pre-agreed, but there is *gharar* in the claim amount. Therefore *gharar* exists in all insurance contracts, either in premiums or in claims. In Islamic insurance, scholars agree that engaging in *takaful* transactions, with a donation element as part of their contribution, offsets *gharar*.

Maysir (Gambling)

Some arguments against conventional insurance are based on the grounds that insurance contracts are basically gambling contracts. Islam rejects any contract where financial gain comes from chance or speculation. Insurance, however, needs to comply with the principle of insurable interest. This principle requires a financial and legal relationship between the insured and the subject matter of insurance. The insured is only entitled to get a claim if he proves his insurable interest, and this feature therefore nullifies the notion that insurance is a gamble.

The other difference between gambling and insurance is that the first is a speculative risk (which is uninsurable), while the latter consists of pure risk only (i.e., the insured should not make a gain but should be put back into the same financial position as before the loss occurred).

The Concept of Islamic Insurance

The first Islamic insurance company was set up in Sudan in 1979. Today there are many Islamic insurance operators in Muslim as well as non-Muslim countries. The main concept of Islamic insurance is that it is an alternative to conventional insurance, with characteristics and features that comply with *shariah* requirements. This is done by eliminating the objections against conventional insurance. "The term *takaful* is an infinitive noun which is derived from the Arabic root verb *kafal'* or *kafala*, meaning to guarantee or bear responsibility for" (Kassar *et al.*, 2008, p. 26).

The main features of Islamic insurance are:

- cooperative risk sharing by using charitable donations to eliminate *gharar* and *riba*;

- clear financial segregation between the participant (insured) and the operator (insurance company);

- *shariah*-compliant underwriting policies and investment strategies.

Cooperative Risk-Sharing

The characteristics of a cooperative include self-responsibility, democracy, equality, equity, solidarity, honesty, openness, social responsibility, and caring for others. While mutuality or cooperative risk-sharing is at the core of Islamic insurance, it cannot alone create an Islamic insurance operation. Islamic insurance is based on more than one contractual relationship: the first relationship is a mutual insurance contract between policyholders (contributors) and each other. This is similar to a pure mutual insurance relationship, taking into consideration the concept of donation *(tabarru)* instead of premiums and an ethical framework of Islamic transactions. The main features behind cooperative insurance are as follows.

- Policyholders pay premiums to a cooperative fund with the intention of it being a donation to those who will suffer losses *(tabarru)*.

- Policyholders are entitled to receive any surplus resulting from the operation of the cooperative insurance fund.

- Policyholders are liable to make up for any deficits that result from the operation of the cooperative insurance fund.

- The amount of contribution (premium) differs from one participant to another, based on the degree of risk in general insurances and actuarial principles in life assurance.

- There is no unified system to operate the treatment of surplus and deficit. There is therefore more than one model accepted by *shariah* scholars being used in practice.

Clear Segregation between Participant and Operator

In conventional insurance, the insurance company is a profit-making organization that aims to maximize profit by accepting the financial burden of others' losses. The insurance company is owned by shareholders who are entitled to receive any profit and are responsible for financing any deficit. Under Islamic insurance, the system is that the insurance company's role is restricted to managing the portfolio and investing the insurance contributions for and on behalf of the participants. The relationship between the participants and the insurance company (as an operator, not as an insurer) is different. There are four different models in operation: The *mudarabh* model, the *wakalah* model, the hybrid *mudarabh–wakalah* model, and the pure cooperative model (non-profit). "The overarching goal of Takaful is brotherhood, solidarity, protection and mutual cooperation between members" (Kassar *et al.*, 2008, p. 66).

Shariah-Compliant Policies and Strategies

Ethical insurers invest money in a responsible way in industries that are ethically sound and do not harm the environment or people. Islamic insurance is similar, except that the ethical considerations are extended to those which do not contravene the religion of Islam and are monitored by a *shariah* board, which is part of the company structure. In particular, the investment and underwriting policies need to be free of any involvement with the prohibited activities of gambling, alcohol, pork, armaments, tobacco, and interest-bearing activities, loans, and securities.

Case Study

American Insurance Group

The potential for *takaful* business is evidenced by the fact that almost all new insurance license applications in the Middle East region are for *takaful* companies. Even many Western insurers, such as American Insurance Group (AIG), have realized the potential of *takaful* and have set up their own *takaful* operations. AIG Takaful, known as Enaya, which means "care," was established in 2006 in Bahrain with a US$15 million paid-up capital and licensed by the Central Bank of Bahrain. Enaya's plan was to start business in the Gulf region and then expand into the Far East and Europe.

Conclusion

Islamic insurance has grown out of the need of many stakeholders in the Islamic world to have protection for assets and liabilities. This protection was required in a similar fashion to that provided by conventional insurance which, for a variety of reasons, was often viewed as prohibited in Islam. *Takaful* or Islamic insurers have been structured in such a way that Islamic scholars are satisfied that the main objections to insurance, which are *riba*, *gharar*, and *maysir*, have been addressed.

Summary and Further Steps

Islamic insurance is the fastest-growing area of insurance throughout the world, including in Western countries. In order to call a company Islamic, there are features that need to be built into the structure:

- cooperative risk-sharing, by using charitable donations to eliminate *gharar* and *riba*;

- clear financial segregation between the participant (insured) and the operator (insurance company);

- *shariah*-compliant underwriting policies and investment strategies.

More Info

Books:

El-Gamal, Mahmoud Amin. *A Basic Guide to Contemporary Islamic Banking and Finance*. Houston, TX: Rice University, 2000.

Jaffer, Sohail (ed). *Islamic Insurance: Trends, Opportunities and the Future of Takaful*. London: Euromoney Books, 2007.

Kassar, Khaled, Omar Clark Fisher, *et al*. *What's Takaful—A Guide to Islamic Insurance*. Beirut: BISC Group, 2008.

Ma'sum Billah, M. *Islamic Insurance (Takaful)*. Kuala Lumpur: Ilmiah Publishers, 2003.

Websites:

Institute of Islamic Banking and Finance: www.islamic-banking.com

Islamic Banking and Finance: www.islamicbankingandfinance.com

Middle East Insurance Review: www.meinsurancereview.com